Sexual States of Mind

"Sexual States of Mind" sets out to revise the psycho-analytical theory of sexuality, as formulated by Freud in the "Three Essays on Sexuality" and the later theory of narcissism, in the light of the Structural Theory which he developed in the 20's. In so doing, the original nebulous formulation of the infantile polymorphous-perverse disposition and genetic concepts of stages of psycho-sexual development and erogenous zone primacies eventuating in a genital primacy and pregenital foreplay is shown to resolve itself. Through delineation of the distinction between adult and infantile structures of the mind and their characterological foundation on introjective versus narcissistic modes of identification, criteria of a purely psycho-analytical variety are evolved for assessing the significance of sexual states of mind and consequent behaviour.

Upon this foundation, Dr. Meltzer then reconstructs the theory of perversions in a manner which lends itself to clearcut application to the consulting room as well as providing a theoretical framework for using psycho-analytical findings for work in allied fields of aesthetics, pedagogy, law and politics. The economic principles of the paranoid-schizoid and depressive positions, as described by Melanie Klein, are shown to foster a more precise ethical position in relation to sexual behaviour than the more hedonistic one implied by Freud's pleasure and reality principles. The outcome is a theory which binds together emotion, meaning and value in a comprehensive approach to sexual behaviour and phantasy.

The Roland Harris Trust

SEXUAL
STATES
OF
MIND

Donald Meltzer M.D.

CLUNIE PRESS
Perthshire · Scotland

SBN 902965 02 6

First published 1973
Reprinted 1979
Reprinted 1990

Acknowledgements

AMONG the many people—patients, students, colleagues and friends —who have helped me to frame the concepts contained in this volume, I must single out those whose special encouragement and assistance with the preparation of the manuscript and book carried me on: Mrs Esther Bick, Miss Patti Koock, Mr Roger Money-Kryle, Mrs Elizabeth Bott Spillius, Mr Adrian Stokes, Miss Doreen Weddell.

The Roland Harris Trust Library No 2

Printed in Great Britain by
Billing & Sons Ltd, Worcester

Table of Contents

Introduction

It is with a sense of some urgency that the formation of this book was undertaken. This sense of urgency includes the field of psycho-analysis and its practice as well as unease about the part that psych-analytical findings have played in the present state of confusion regarding sexuality, which confronts us on every side today.

No one can doubt that the great advances of medical science in combating venereal disease have furthered the release of sexual behaviour from the fear-ridden restraint imposed upon it by religion-inspired morality. And more recent developments in medicine promise release from ethical concerns through foolproof contracep-tion. It is ironic that the science which was so revolutionary in respect to sexual bigotry should now find itself so "puritanical" in respect of sexual licence. But where the pendulum of ignorance swings wide, psycho-analysis stands firm on its philosophical foundations of belief in individuality, of the primacy of psychic reality, and therefore of the concreteness of responsibility. It is bound to view all statistical concepts of normality, as it will view all sociological concepts of culture, as hypocritical or even cynical evasions of responsibility when they are put forward as causal explanation of human behaviour. It must be equally suspicious of cosmic mysticism.

But it has a mysticism of its own, as does all science which has not arrogantly left the rails, namely that the plumbing of the mysteries of the universe never intends to answer the ultimate question and destroy our awe and wonder. Rather, science seeks to discover and not to invade the sanctuaries of nature, to enhance our humility while augmenting our self-control—not our control of the universe, but our self-control, in order that we may carry the responsibility which the evolution of mind has laid upon us. As we can now meddle with everything on earth, we are now the earth's custodians. And it is too late to try to expel God-the-father from our inner world by elegant socio-political theories, in order for him to resume these burdens.

So much for the urgency in which this book was, as I say, forced. Its content is a tribute to the line of genius which runs from Freud,

through Abraham to Melanie Klein to Wilfred Bion. Where they
have shown the direction, the details must be filled in by others in
order to forge the tools which can implement their great insights.
In what follows I have only seldom referred to the work of other
people, psycho-analysts, philosophers, biologists, sociologists,
anthropologists or others. Where I do it is not for the sake of
"credits" but to direct readers for further study or to quote a
particularly pithy statement of a problem. There is no possibility of
apportioning credit for one's realisations. But a seldom-mentioned
area of credit is useful to indicate here, as it adds a facet to the
conception of the psycho-analytical method whose findings are laid
out. A particular analysis begins with a relatively ill person coming
to a relatively well one for help. But if the effort to organise and set
in motion a "psycho-analytical process" succeeds, the two people are
caught up in an intimacy, a frankness, a revelation of thought and
feeling whose intensity, I assert, is unparalleled. It compounds the
depth of concentration of the breast-feeding mother and babe, the
passion of the coital couple, the artist's urgency to give plastic form
to experience, the impulse toward verbalisation of the philosopher,
and the craving for precision of the mathematician—potentially.
When a particular analysis catches fire and new insights are made
possible, it does so by the interaction of the two minds.

It would only be just, then, that the patients whose material is
used to illustrate the various concepts described in what follows
should be given an acknowledgment. Some day this may be possible.
But where the privacy of our patients still needs protection against
bigotry, we may make a beginning by acknowledging the obvious,
that every psycho-analytical discovery is a self-revelation and every
paper an autobiography. So at least the name of one of the patients
is revealed.

This clarifies the differentiation between credit and responsibility.
In what follows I believe the implications for a correct understanding
of sexuality contained in the line of work Freud-Abraham-Klein-
Bion is faithfully and correctly traced. The responsibility for this
"correctness" must lie with the author. If it is a correct theory it is
"theirs", if it is wrong it is "mine". But of course the inability to see
anything original in one's own work is due to the residual confusion
between internal and external as regards the genesis of one's own
super-ego-ideal. For, after all, who would willingly be an orphan!

The plan of the book is a simple one. The history of the psycho-
analytical theory of psychosexual development and clinical sexual
psycho-pathology is presented in the form of lectures given at the
Institute of Education, University of London, 1964 and 1965, and
two given at the Institute of Psycho-analysis, 1968–69, respectively.

They vary in their degree of sophistication and presupposed knowledge of the literature.

Next the revision of the theory of psychosexual development is presented. The composition of the super-ego-ideal and its position in the sexual life in particular (Chapter 10) is then elucidated.

The way is then clear for the revision of the theory of sexual psychopathology in respect of several dimensions of differentiation—adult-infantile (Chapters 11–12), polymorphism-perversity (Chapters 12–13), perverse sexuality-sexual perversion (Chapters 15–16–18). Problems of clinical practice related to ambisexuality (Chapter 16), the addictive transference (Chapter 19) and the place of work in sexuality (Chapter 17) are investigated.

Finally, some exploration is undertaken into the implications and applications of this revised theory to other areas such as Politics (Chapters 20–21), Education (Chapter 22), Abortion (Chapter 23), Law (Chapter 24).

Since various Chapters date from 1960 onwards, where my current views are different from those expressed in the body of the Chapter, footnotes have been added.

It is purely a psycho-analytical work in that it risks everything on the validity of the psycho-analytical method of observation. This validity is most likely to be felt emotionally by those who have known the method at first hand. To assist the intellectual grasp of those readers who are acquainted with the psycho-analytical literature, it might be worth while to mention two items, one regarding technical language, the other pertaining to the general theory.

A general notational system for describing clinical phenomena is followed which is the same as that used in *The Psycho-analytical Process* as regards the naming of part and whole objects, parts of self, erogenous zones and zonal confusions. Thus the objects of infantile phantasy, whether internal or external, are referred to in infantile terms—"mummy", "daddy", "mummy's breast", "daddy's penis", etc. indicating whole- or part-object states. Further functional divisions of part-objects are indicated by elision—"toilet-breast", "feeding-breast", "inside-penises", "nipple-penis", etc. Parts of the infantile self are described by sexual differentiation, good-bad distinction and level of development—"baby-part", "boy-" or "girl-part", "good parts", "bad" or "destructive part". The terms "adult" and "infantile" are used exclusively in a metapsychological sense, while "grown-up" and "childish" describe external behaviour or cultural values.

The theory to be described and exemplified is an elaboration and extension of the *Three Essays on Sexuality* in the light of structural theory and the Kleinian developments. In brief, Freud's conception of infantile sexuality as "polymorphously perverse" is separated into polymorphism and perversity, which are bound firmly to psychic structure. By this means we can explore problems of narcissistic organisation and trace their influences both upon development and regressive disorders. Further, by means of the concept of introjective identification on the one hand and an integrated conception of the super-ego-ideal the category of genitality is expanded into one of *adult sexuality*, which is metapsychologically rather than descriptively distinguished from *infantile sexuality*. This theory implies that, while in infantile sexuality states of mind reflect a direct (1°) relation of Ego to Id, in adult sexual states an indirect (2°) relation exists mediated through the introjective identification with the sexual union of the internal combined object (super-ego-ideal). Upon this groundwork the general field of clinical phenomena related to sexual states of mind is given a new organisation and some specific contributions are made to the metapsychology of perversions, addictions, fetishism, and regressive illness in general. It will be apparent that, throughout, in both theoretical formulations and clinical examples, the primal scene or phantasy, in an expanded form, is held as the frame of reference for the description of all sexual states of mind, both adult and infantile.

Part I
HISTORY

SECTION A

THE THEORY OF PSYCHOSEXUAL DEVELOPMENT*

* Adapted from lectures read at the Institute of Education, University of London, 1964-65.

CHAPTER 1

The Psycho-Analytical Method and its Theories

IN a volume of this sort I can hardly aspire to present a comprehensive picture of what must surely be the most complex problem in science, one to which nearly every branch of science and the humanities may be expected to make some contribution, each unique according to its methods and materials. While interests and training as biologist, doctor and psychiatrist may extend my range, I must yet admit that my only field of special knowledge and wide experience is in psycho-analysis. I wish you to see in the apology a reference to the narrowness of psycho-analysis, its methods and its discoveries.

Since the value of the findings of any scientific discipline can only be judged on the basis of an understanding of its methods and materials, I wish to outline briefly the history of the psycho-analytic method for investigating the workings of the human mind. By differentiating between psycho-analytical discoveries and psycho-analytic theories, one can adopt a reasonable position of judgement as to the validity of what follows under two distinct categories: (a) evaluation of the reliability of the data for the reconstruction of the developmental history of individual patients; (b) critical judgement on the quality of thought which has entered into the construction of theories about child development from these clinical findings.

I do not intend to discuss the many avenues outside clinical psycho-analysis that trained psycho-analysts have pursued in their legitimate desire to enrich, corroborate or extend psycho-analytic findings. The fields of infant observation, ethology, psychological testing, work in nurseries or special schools, anthropology—these and many others have played a role in the evolution of psycho-analysis, but are not considered here.

Sigmund Freud, working in the cosmopolitan atmosphere of turn-of-the-century Vienna, coming from a non-orthodox and relatively assimilated Jewish family background, with training as a physician, neurologist and research worker in neuro-physiology, found himself fascinated by the work of Charcot in Paris using hypnosis and by Breuer's work in Vienna with hysterical patients. By means of hypnosis, then later a method of forced association and finally free association, Freud set about establishing the first working

5

concept of the unconcious as the determining factor in the formation of the pathological symptoms of the hysterical patient. But he
did something else at the same time, and herein lies his greatness and
the essence of the psycho-analytical method: he began to investigate
himself, both in the light of his discoveries with his patients and in
respect of his emotional responses to his patients.

The first of these two seeming side-lines of investigation produced
such cornerstones of psycho-analytic insight as *The Interpretation
of Dreams* (1899), *The Psychopathology of Everyday Life* (1901), and
Wit and its Relation to the Unconscious (1905). The second of these
sidelines developed into a systematic self-analysis of which you will
find some account in Ernest Jones' biography of Freud. This
capacity for rigorous self-scrutiny enabled Freud to continue the
work with hysterics following the initial joint publication, *Studies in
Hysteria* (1895), with Joseph Breuer, while the latter was put off by
the first full-blown erotic transference which a female patient
developed to him. It was the truly heroic effort of self-analysis,
begun in 1897 and presumably continued as part of his daily life to
the time of his death in London in 1939, which laid the foundation of
the psycho-analytical method. By means of the systematic inquiry
into the nature and origins of his own emotional and phantasy
response to his patients' productions, or what he soon came to call
the countertransference, Freud was able to erect as the keystone of
psycho-analytic investigation the concept of the transference. This
he presented formally fifteen years later in his paper "The Dynamics
of the Transference" (1912). It remains the essence of the psycho-
analytical method, and the only feature by which it can claim a place
of its own among the battery of techniques deployed to plumb the
mysteries of the human psyche.

What, then, is *The Transference?* Here is Freud's own description
of the drama of the transference as he saw it at that time: "The
unconscious impulses do not want to be remembered in the way the
treatment desires them to be, but endeavour to reproduce themselves
in accordance with the timelessness of the unconscious and its
capacity for hallucination. Just as happens in dreams, the patient
regards the products of the awakening of his unconscious impulses
as contemporaneous and real; he seeks to put his passions . . ."
(both love and hate, he has already explained) ". . . info action
without taking any account of the real situation. The doctor tries
to compel him to fit these emotional impulses into the nexus of the
treatment and of his life-history, to submit them to intellectual
consideration and to understand them in the light of their psychical
value."[1]

[1] Freud, "The Dynamics of the Transference", *S.E.*, Vol. XII, p. 108.

Two years earlier, in 1910, Freud had already made explicit his conviction that the analyst's capacity to comprehend the unconscious phantasy and emotion bound up in the patient's *transference* depended on his contact with his own unconscious response to "emotional impulses", the *countertransference*. He writes of it thus: "We have become aware of the 'countertransference' which arises (in the analyst) as a result of the patient's influence on his unconscious feelings, and we are almost inclined to insist that he shall recognise this countertransference in himself and overcome it. Now that a considerable number of people are practising psycho-analysis and exchanging their observations with one another, we have noticed that no psycho-analyst goes further than his own complexes and internal resistances permit; and we consequently require that he shall begin his activity with a self-analysis and continually carry it deeper while he is making his observations on his patients. Anyone who fails to produce results in a self-analysis of this kind may at once give up any idea of being able to treat patients by analysis."[1]

However, Freud's view of the adequacy of his own self-analysis and of the ubiquity of the potential for self-analysis among his followers became less sanguine as the years passed. While in 1909 he could blithely answer the question of how one could become an analyst with the reply, "by analysing one's own dreams",[2] only three years later (1912) he wrote with conviction of the need for the "training analysis". "Anyone who takes up the work" (of analysis) "seriously should choose this course" (analysis by someone with expert knowledge) "which offers more than one advantage; the sacrifice involved in laying oneself open to another person without being driven to it by illness is amply rewarded. Not only is one's aim of learning to know what is hidden in one's own mind far more rapidly attained and with less expense of affect" (than by self-analysis) "but impressions and convictions will be gained in relation to oneself which will be sought in vain from studying books and attending lectures."[3]

This does not imply that he had swung to the view that training-analysis enabled one to dispense with self-analysis. Rather, he had recognised that self-analysis was really possible as a successful and continuing process only when begun through analysis with another person. Thus "Anyone who can appreciate the high value of self-knowledge and increase in self-control thus acquired will, when it" (the formal analysis) "is over, continue the analytic examination of

---

[1] Freud. *S.E.*, XI, 144
[2] Freud, *S.E.*, XI, 33
[3] Freud, *S.E.*, XII, 116

his personality in the form of self-analysis, and be content to realise that, within himself as well as in the external world, he must always expect to find something new."[1]

In the half-century since that was written, as the demand for analytic treatment has driven forward the need for analytic training, the so-called "training analysis" has taken its place as the keystone of the training process. As psycho-analytic treatment has increased its scope from its original preoccupation with hysterical symptoms to the entire gamut of emotional and mental illness and character disorder, so also has it increased the depth and intensity of self-scrutiny required of analysts. The training requirements, especially for long and intensive analysis, have increased. This is due also to a parallel development in technique, for as the transference process has been carried deeper into the mind to levels linked to the earliest years and even months of life, the preverbal experience and memories of the individual have come into focus. But recognition of these phenomena depends very greatly on the psycho-analyst's contact with, and control over, his countertransference. Much of the important work in this area has grown up here in London, under the stimulus of the discoveries of Melanie Klein, by such workers as Donald Winnicott, Paula Heimann and Wilfred Bion.[2] The latter has traced some of the earliest modes of mental functioning between child and mother by means of investigation of the countertransfer-ence. He writes in *Learning from Experience:* "The activity we know as 'thinking' was in origin a procedure for unburdening the psyche of accretions of stimuli and the mechanism is that which has been described by Melanie Klein as projective identification. The broad outline of this theory is that there exists an omnipotent phantasy that it is possible to split off temporarily undesired, though sometimes valued, parts of the personality and put them into an object. In practice, it is possible, and desirable in the interests of beneficial therapy, to observe and interpret the evidence that supports this theory and which this theory explains in a way that no other theory does.

"It is also possible, and in fact essential, to observe evidence which shows that a patient in whom the operation of this omnipotent phantasy can be deduced is capable of behaviour which is related to a counterpart in reality of this phantasy. The patient, even at the outset of life, has contact with reality sufficient to enable him to act

[1] *Ibid.*, 117

[2] At that time I was not aware of how systematic and penetrating had been the studies in this area carried on by the late Heinrich Racker of Buenos Aires. See his book *Transference and Countertransference*, Int. Psa. Library No. 73. London Hogarth Press, 1968.

in a way that *engenders in the mother feelings that he does not want, or which he wants his mother to have.*"[1]

In these last few words you have a statement of one of the most advanced outposts of psycho-analytical research today. Much of what follows must be evaluated in terms of the possible validity of this theory, in operational form: when the infantile transference to the analyst begins to reproduce patterns of object relationships derived from the patient's earliest months of life, both his capacity to communicate with the analyst and his capacity to obtain relief from unbearable psychic pains revived by the analytic process depend on one primitive mental mechanism. This mechanism, projective identification, works by a phantasy of being able to split off a part of the self containing the state of mind which is either to be communicated or to be evacuated. This part of the self is, in phantasy, put into the analyst (originally into the parent figure). Not only does this occur in phantasy but also it can engender modes of feeling which actually have a congruent temporary effect on the behaviour of a receptive figure in the outside world.

Thus it is Dr Bion's theory that the mother can understand her baby through her unconscious receptiveness to the baby's projective identification and that the analyst who is sufficiently in touch with his own unconscious can be aware of a similar receptivity and responsiveness in himself. Notice that he must first of all be sufficiently receptive and then secondly be sufficiently in touch with the unconscious processes in himself which result from this receptivity. By this second step he is able to respond analytically rather than parentally.

Here then is the history of the development of the psycho-analytical method for investigating the human mind. As I have stressed, its only claim to uniqueness is its basic tool, the investigation of the transference. Its only claim to validity is the accuracy of its instrument of observation, the analysed mind of the psycho-analyst, his contact with his countertransference and his capacity to think about it. You can thus see that psycho-analysis operates, as does any scientific process, by placing an instrument within the system to be observed and that it requires all data to be evaluated in respect of the alteration in the original system brought about by the introduction of the instrument of observation.

But this method of collecting data is only the foundation of psycho-analysis as a method of inquiry. We must now turn to the nature of the data it collects, and to its manner of formulating and testing hypotheses. Never has psycho-analysis claimed to be an inductive

---

[1] Wilfred Bion, *Learning from Experience*, (London, Heinemann, 1962), p. 31.

system. Such claims by other branches of science have been strongly challenged by recent developments in the philosophy of science (see Popper). The unconscious process, or as Medawar calles it, the "inspirational" process, of hypothesis formation is at its core. In the psycho-analytical method this manifests itself as a constant function called *interpretation*. While observing the transference and the countertransference, the analyst will occasionally, even frequently, offer to his patient a tentative hypothesis regarding the nature of the object relationship going on in the treatment room at that moment. This is his fundamental activity, his specific therapeutic type of intervention. True, he creates a setting, he accepts communications and projections: these are all more or less accomplished by self-control— a negative element. The analyst's positive contribution is the interpretation, by means of which he hopes to bring a fluid state of affairs of feeling and phantasy into more defined structure available for intellectual judgement. Or it may do nothing. Or it may increase the chaos. But one of these three it must do, and subsequent observation should elicit which. When a similar state of improved order has been brought about by a particular formulation repeatedly, over months and years, its validity can be said to be established. Conviction develops in patient and analyst alike regarding its validity as a working hypothesis which brings an increase of order into the patient's mental processes.[1]

Psycho-analysis, then, in addition to being a scientific deductive system,[2] is also an experimental method utilising predictive validation as its chief mode of verification of data. It is one thing more, and this is what most concerns students of child development. It constructs theories of past events on the basis of a great assumption, called by Freud the "repetition compulsion". First mentioned in 1910 but not really put forward as a principle of mental functioning until 1920 in "Beyond the Pleasure Principle" (*S.E.*, Vol. XVIII, Ch. III and IV) it has come to be the theoretical basis of all psychoanalytic reconstruction of the individual patient's early history and,

[1] These ideas were later developed further in my book, *The Psycho-analytical Process*, London, Heinemann, 1967.
[2] I would no longer hold this view but rather see that inductive and deductive method have a varying balance and interplay in the work of different people. Freud himself, I realise, was able to work in an oscillating way, pressed by inspired hypotheses to extend his method, which in turn threw up new data which required new hypotheses. The great structural revision of the 1920–26 period illustrates this flux, containing a revision of old statements (Ego and the Id) pressed upon him by the phenomenology of narcissism and by a newly inspired hypothesis ("Beyond the Pleasure Principle") that contained the methodological tool which was to open up the problem of masochism and the perversions (see Chapters 5 and 6).

by implication and extrapolation to anthropology and paleontology, the pre-history of the species.

Drawing upon such diverse phenomenon as the transference, the play of children and the dreams of patients with traumatic neurosis, Freud posited a "compulsion to repeat" as a driving force in the psyche "beyond the pleasure principle", *i.e.* more primitive even than the economic concerns with pleasure and pain. In one of his most brilliant and controversial passages he writes: "But how is the predicate of being 'instinctual' related to the compulsion to repeat? At this point we cannot escape a suspicion that we may have come upon the track of a universal attribute of instincts and perhaps of organic life in general, which has not hitherto been clearly recognised or at least not explicitly stressed. *It seems, then, that an instinct is an urge inherent in organic life to restore an earlier state of things* which the living entity has been obliged to abandon under pressure of external disturbing forces; that is, it is a kind of organic elasticity, or, to put it another way, the expression of the inertia inherent in organic life."[1]

In practice, this means that so great is the urge to repeat past configurations of experience that they will force their way upon the scene whenever the impediments to their doing so are removed. They do so in sleep, fatigue, intoxication, hypnosis, brain injury, and, in an orderly way which makes their systematic study possible, in the psycho-analytic transference, when the anxieties blocking them have been gradually and painstakingly removed by interpretation. Their appearance in analysis in relation to the conflicts of the early childhood oedipal period was named by Freud "the transference neurosis". The deeper and earlier configurations which can now be approached have been correspondingly named by Herbert Rosenfeld "the transference psychosis". (See *Psychotic States*, Int. Psa. Library No. 65, 1956.)

To summarise, then: first of all, psycho-analysis has a very limited field of study—the unconscious object relations—to which it can lay any special claim of methodological superiority. Its method is to establish a two person relationship in a very controlled setting and to study the events that transpire when the analyst, a person trained in special sensitivity to other people and possessing a deep contact with his own unconscious, limits his activity as much as possible to *interpretation of the transference*. These interpretations are hypotheses whose validity he tests by predictive means and whose accuracy and complexity he augments by serial approximation.

On the basis of such validated hypotheses about the here-and-

<hr/>

[1] Freud "Beyond the Pleasure Principle" *S.E.*, Vol. XVIII, p. 36.

now transference and using his inference from the theory of the compulsion to repeat, the analyst may reconstruct the *development of the unconscious object relations of the patient.* From a wide experience of individual patients he may then generalise and propose a theory· of development which he believes to be biologically founded on the deep levels of the psyche and not fundamentally different in varying cultures, races, or circumstances of life.

CHAPTER 2

Childhood Sexuality and the Oedipus Complex

IN Chapter 1 I have outlined the historical development of the psycho-analytic method for investigating the human psyche, in order to help in evaluating the validity of the reconstruction of infant and child development which is now to follow. The main points I made were that the method is unique in its chief instrument—the analysed mind of the psycho-analyst; in its data—the development of the transference; in its experimental design—the use of interpretation as a variable in the two-person relationship; and in its theoretical basis for reconstruction—the concept of the repetition compulsion. But I also stressed that it pays for this uniqueness by the narrowness of its special field of study, namely unconscious object relations.

In these next three Chapters I have elected once more to follow historical chronology—the evolution of psycho-analytic theory about development—rather than ontogenetic chronology, for indeed in a sense the two are necessarily inversely related to one another. I plan first to discuss the scientific discovery by Freud of childhood sexuality and of the Oedipus complex as a genital conflict. In Chapter 3 I will outline the discoveries relevant to the pregenital development, especially from weaning onward, much of which is implicit in the work of Karl Abraham. In the fourth Chapter I will present the reconstruction of the earliest post-natal period, from birth to weaning, along with the revision of our conception of later development which it has made necessary. This is very largely the outcome of the researches of Melanie Klein and of still more recent work with psychotic adults and children.

In Freud's written work prior to the appearance of the *Three Essays on Sexuality* in 1905 (*S.E.*, Vol. VII) the existence of sexuality as a powerful force in the minds of children is mooted over and over again. The Oedipus complex is outlined as early as 1900 in *The Interpretation of Dreams*. But these were, in many ways, contributions to psychopathology. Not until the famous *Three Essays* did he assert the ubiquity, and therefore the essential "normality" of these phenomena. Protest as we may, a certain blasé acceptance of the changes in our culture has dulled our sense of the momentous significance of these findings and of the impact they have had on every branch of the humanities, the law, morality, religion, child rearing, education and art. One must read Jones' biography to recall the isolation, abuse, deprivation and neglect which Freud reaped for his reward in those early years.

His findings were derived from two sources, essentially: the psycho-analytical treatment of neurotics, especially hysterics, and his self-analysis. He concluded the following: that sexual preoccupations and activities were an ubiquitous phenomenon in early childhood, reaching a crescendo at the height of the Oedipus conflict somewhere between three and five years; that this sexuality was in essence "polymorphous" and "perverse" with increasing concentration on the genitals; that the period of maximum conflict was followed by a period of relative "latency" of the sexual drives, fractured at puberty by the eruption attending the maturation of the organs of reproduction. Although Freud's views about the differences of male and female development were modified somewhat in later years and although the important conception of narcissism entered as a differential in regard to the object relatedness of the sexual drives, his view of childhood sexuality remained broadly as stated in 1905. Consider a portion of the summary to the *Three Essays*, with changes added in 1915, 1920 and 1924. It gives a vivid picture of the growth of Freud's thought, just as it highlights the more controversial issues which I will discuss further and which will come under scrutiny again in subsequent Chapters. He writes: "We found it a regrettable thing that the existence of the sexual instinct in childhood has been denied and that the sexual manifestations not infrequently to be observed in children have been described as irregularities. It seemed to us on the contrary that children bring germs of sexual activity with them into the world, that they already enjoy sexual satisfaction when they begin to take nourishment and that they persistently seek to repeat the experience in the familiar activity of "thumb sucking". The sexual activity of children, however, does not, it appears, develop *pari passu* with their other functions, but, after a short period of efflorescence . . ." ("from the ages of three to five", Freud added in 1915, changed in 1920 to read "from two to five") ". . . after a short period of efflorescence from the ages of two to five, enters upon the so-called period of latency. During that period the production of sexual excitement is not by any means stopped but continues and produces a store of energy which is employed to a great extent for purposes other than sexual—namely, on the one hand in contributing the sexual components to social feelings and on the other hand (through repression and reaction-forming) in building up the subsequently developed barriers against sexuality."[1]

[1] Freud, *Three Essays on Sexuality*, S.E., Vol. VII, p. 232.

I break Freud's commentary here to point out that he clearly does *not* put forward, as has so often been attributed to him, that development of the sexual *drives* is diphasic, with peaks in the oedipal and pubertal periods, but that the sexual *activities* are diphasic. There is *no* evidence of a diphasic biological development, as far as endocrine studies can determine. To return to Freud: "On this view, the forces destined to retain the sexual instinct upon certain lines are built up in childhood chiefly at the cost of perverse sexual impulses and with the assistance of education. A certain proportion of the infantile sexual impulses would seem to evade these uses and succeed in expressing itself as sexual activity. We next found that sexual excitement in children springs from a multiplicity of forces. Satisfaction arises first and foremost from the appropriate sensory excitation of what we have described as erotogenic zones. It seems probable that any part of the skin and any sense-organ" ("probably, indeed, *any* organ", he added in 1915, including in his schema sensations inside the body related to internal processes) "can function as an erotogenic zone, though there are some particularly marked erotogenic zones whose excitations would seem to be secured from the very first by certain organic contrivances. It further appears that sexual excitation is a by-product, as it were, of a large number of processes that occur in the organism, as soon as they reach a certain degree of intensity, and most especially of any relatively powerful emotion, even though it is of a distressing nature."

It can be seen that Freud is here already reaching toward the concept of masochism which was finally formulated in his paper "The Economic Problem of Masochism" (1924—19 years after the *Three Essays*). He continues: "The excitations from all these sources are not yet combined, but each follows its own separate aim, which is merely the attainment of a certain sort of pleasure. In childhood, therefore, the sexual instinct is without any object, that is, auto-erotic." In 1920 this was amended to read, "In childhood, therefore, the sexual instinct is *not unified and is at first* without any object, that is, auto-erotic". He has not stated his view of the duration of this auto-erotism. You can see, however, that Freud was tending with the years to view the child's sexuality as more and more bound to object relations and less "narcissistic" by nature. This is the most vital point of departure for later theories of infantile development, elaborated in the following Chapters.

He continues: "The erotogenic zone of the genitals begins to make itself noticeable, it seems, even during the years of childhood. This may happen in two ways. Either, like any other erotogenic zone, it yields satisfaction in response to appropriate sensory stimulation, or, in a manner which is not quite understandable, when satisfaction is derived from other sources, a sexual excitation is simultaneously produced which has a special relation to the genital area. We were reluctantly obliged to admit that we could not satisfactorily explain the relation between sexual excitation and sexual satisfaction, or that between the activity of the genital zone and the activity of other sources of sexuality."

This is the point at which he stopped in 1905. Not until fifteen years later, in the 1920 edition, was he able to add the two paragraphs which adumbrate the modern developments in psycho-analytic theory. This is what he added: "We found from the study of neurotic disorders that beginnings of an organisation of the sexual instinctual components can be detected in the sexual life of children from its very beginning. During a first, very early phase, oral erotism occupies most of the picture. A second of these pregenital organisations is characterised by the predominance of sadism and anal erotism. It is not until a third phase has been reached that the genital zones proper contribute their share in determining sexual life . . ." Four years later, 1924, he concluded this sentence with the clause, "and in children this last phase is developed only so far as to a primacy of the phallus. . . ." meaning that he felt male and female sexuality to be undifferentiated as yet, all subsumed under pre-occupation with the penis. Vaginal masturbation and the desire for babies he considered pre-pubertal development, a point of major disagreement with more recent findings.

Here then is the position Freud had reached in 1905, with the amendments of 1915, 1920 and 1924. I wish to pause to discuss these findings for a few moments before going into more detail regarding Freud's views of the Oedipus complex and its relation to the establishment of the institution of conscience or super-ego as described in 1924; and of Freud's final views on female sexuality as formulated in his 1931 paper. He had come laboriously to the view that sexuality, distributed among the erotogenic zones of the inside and outside of the body, but increasingly concentrated in leading zones of contact, real and phantasied, with external objects, chiefly the parents, could be seen to form itself into what he called "organisations of the libido" at different periods of the child's development. The idea of objectless auto-erotism was amended in 1914 by the concept of narcissism, in which the infant and child was seen to take parts of its own body as object of its sexual impulses. As we shall see in the next Chapter, Freud later divided this into primary and secondary narcissism, the former a shrinking concept of a pre-object phase of development in earliest infancy, the validity of which has since been challenged. The secondary narcissism was then seen as an erotic attachment to parts of the body, or later of the personality, identified with, or as a substitute for, objects, undertaken as a defence against deprivation (as for instance during separation) or anxiety.

These early organisations of sexuality and object relations Freud recognised as being distinct one from the other in many ways, not merely in their leading zone, though he named them oral, anal and phallic according to the zonal primacy.   The oral organisation was seen to be led by the mouth, with its object of attachment, the mother's breast, in fact or phantasy.   Its preoccupation was introjective, that is, with the taking in of nourishment and its psychological equivalent, of love.   The anal phase, dominated by the sadism seen to attend the heightened conflicts following weaning, was also conceived to have the mother, more as a whole person, as its object, with the excreta, especially the faeces, as the vehicle of the psychic process of projection, *i.e.* the pushing out of unwanted contents, physical and mental, into an external object.   The phallic phase, not seen as very different in boys and girls, dominated by envy of the father's penis and jealousy over his sexual relation, conceived as "possession" of the mother, appeared to Freud to reach its apogee in the Oedipus complex, at a point of maximal ambivalence.

I stress these views of early mental development, for the next two Chapters will be largely devoted to Abraham's elucidation of the anal phase and Melanie Klein's discoveries, through her direct application of psycho-analysis to young children, of the details of the development of object relations in the pre-weaning period.

But to return to a more detailed description of the Oedipus conflict, as Freud formulated it in his paper "The Dissolution of the Oedipus Complex" in 1924: "To an ever-increasing extent the Oedipus complex reveals its importance as the central phenomenon of the sexual period of early childhood. After that, its dissolution takes place; it succumbs to repression, as we say, and is followed by the latency period. It has not yet become clear, however, what it is that brings about its destruction. Analysis seems to show that it is the experience of painful disappointments. The little girl likes to regard herself as what her father loves above all else; but the time comes when she has to endure a harsh punishment from him and she is cast out of her fool's paradise. The boy regards his mother as his own property; but he finds one day that she has transferred her love and solicitude to a new arrival. Reflection must deepen our sense of the importance of these influences, for it will emphasise the fact that distressing experiences of this sort, which act in opposition to the content of the complex, are inevitable. Even when no special events occur, like those we have mentioned as examples, the absence of the satisfaction hoped for, the continued denial of the desired baby, must in the end lead the small lover to turn away from his hopeless longing. In this way the Oedipus complex would go to its destruction from its lack of success, from the effects of its internal impossibility."[1]

After expressing some ideas about phylogenetic influences, Freud goes on, "We have lately been made more clearly aware than before that a child's sexual development advances to a certain phase at which the genital organ has already taken over the leading role. But the genital is the male one only, or, more correctly, the penis; the female genital has remained undiscovered."

He then expressed his theory about the role of castration anxiety in the normal and pathological destruction of the Oedipus complex. "But", he writes, "there is no evidence to show that, when the threat of castration takes place, these experiences have any effect. It is not until a *fresh* experience comes his way that the child begins to reckon with the possibility of being castrated, and then only hesitantly and unwilling, and not without making efforts to depreciate the significance of something he has himself observed.

"The observation which finally breaks down his unbelief is the sight of the female genitals."

Freud decided that it was this anxiety, the fear of losing the penis in the boy and its corresponding conviction of having lost it in the girl, which opened the way to the abandonment of the primary sexual object, the parent of the opposite sex. But he was not insensible to the complexity of the situation imposed by the bisexual disposition of the child. In the previous year, 1923, in the momentous paper which established our structural view of the psychic apparatus, "The Ego and the Id," he had already seen the complexity. "Closer study usually discloses the more complete Oedipus complex, which is twofold, positive and negative, and is due to the bisexuality originally present in children; that is to say, a boy has not merely an ambivalent attitude toward his father and an affectionate object choice toward his mother, but at the same time he also behaves like a girl and displays an affectionate feminine attitude to the father and a corresponding jealousy and hostility toward his mother."[2]

Freud could recognise that the outcome of this bisexual conflict was the relinquishment of both object choices and the establishment in their place of a new institution in the structure of the mind. *"The broad general outcome of the sexual phase dominated by the Oedipus complex may, therefore, be taken to be the forming of a precipitate in the ego, consisting of these two identifications in some way united with each other. This modification of the ego retains its special position; it confronts the other contents of the ego as an ideal or super-ego."*

[1] "The Dissolution of the Oedipus Complex", *S.E.*, Vol. XIX, p. 173
[2] "The Ego and the Id", *S.E.*, Vol. XIX, p. 33.

Here then is the famous passage which has been the jumping-off place for all the investigation of the last 40 years into the so-called "internal objects", the primitive precursors of conscience or super-ego, whose role in early development and whose perseverance in the deeper levels of the unconscious, were discovered by Melanie Klein and her co-workers to be so crucial for mental health or illness. Those discoveries and their dependence upon Abraham's work will be described in the next two Chapters. To complete this one, we must bring up to date, to its most advanced state, Freud's view of the little girl's development. Up to this point (1924), the male and female child, both bisexual in disposition, were seen to differ only quantitatively in the balance of these innate biological forces. The little girl's vagina was held to be unknown; her clitoris was viewed as phallic in significance and as a source of her sense of inferiority to the boy; and, above all, her femininity was held to contain very little of the castration anxiety which was held to drive the little boy to abandon and dissolve his Oedipus complex. Therefore, Freud writes (XIX, 178): "The fear of castration being thus excluded in the little girl, a powerful motive also drops out for the setting up of a super-ego and for the breaking off of the infantile genital organisation. In her, far more than in the boy, these changes seem to be the result of upbringing and intimidation from outside which threatens her with loss of love."

It can be seen that fidelity to the psycho-analytic method had led Freud to some rather unexpected conclusions about little girls; that, in a sense, they do not know they are female, do not have a conscience, and are directed by their desire for love rather than by any fear of punishment in regard to their oedipal rivalry with their mothers. He himself knew these views were untenable but would have to await further evidence, perhaps evidence collected by female analysts toward whom the maternal transference might more fully unfold itself and who might themselves be more sensitively in touch with the female unconscious, an area where Freud perhaps rightly suspected himself of limitations.

The last significant alteration of his views on the little girl's development came in 1931 in his paper, "Female Sexuality". First he revised his idea of the sequence of events in the little girl, placing her negative (or inverted) Oedipus conflict in a primary position thus: ". . . We can extend the content of the Oedipus complex to include all the child's relations to both parents; or, on the other [hand], we can take due account of our new findings by saying that the female only reaches the normal positive Oedipus situation after she has surmounted a period before it governed by the negative complex. And indeed during that phase a little girl's father is not much else for her than a troublesome rival, although her hostility toward him never reaches the pitch which is characteristic of boys."[1]

The abandoning of this negative pre-oedipal attachment in favour of the positive complex Freud still viewed as driven by disappointment on the one hand and penis-envy on the other. "At some time or other the little girl makes the discovery of her organic inferiority— earlier and more easily, of course, if there are brothers or other boys about. We have already taken a note of the three paths which diverge from this point: (*a*) The one which leads to a cessation of her whole sexual life; (*b*) the one which leads to a defiant over-emphasis of her masculinity, and; (*c*) the first steps toward definitive femininity." (p. 232).

But already his suspicions were aroused that the grievances about not having a penis drew their intensity from far earlier sources of bitterness toward the mother (p. 235), "that her mother did not give her enough milk, did not suckle her long enough". This theme, of the struggle to preserve the good and trusting relation to the breast and mother at weaning forms the armature about which Melanie Klein's reconstruction of the child's development is built, as I shall outline in the fourth Chapter.

One important factor must be kept in mind in evaluating Freud's achievement in this area, namely that Freud came from a 19th century scientific tradition and naturally thought in terms analogous to mechanics, chemistry, and the new archeology of his time. As we move, in the next two Chapters, into the psycho-analytical theories of child development evolved in the past forty years, a change can be seen subtly to appear in the modes of thought and expression, reflecting the impact of the theory of relativity, the second law of thermodynamics in its application to communication and the more catholic view of social structure implicit in modern anthropology. In a word, the model of the mind implicit in psychoanalytic theory will be seen to shift from a hydraulic system (the libido theory) to a communication system, where information rather than energy is mobilised, where order rather than equilibrium is the overrriding principle of organisation, and where the thrust toward development rather than the minimising of tension is seen as the ultimate economic principle.

---

[1] "Female Sexuality", *S.E.*, Vol. XXI, p. 226.

CHAPTER 3

Developmental Phases and Organisational Series

IN the second Chapter, which dealt almost exclusively with the work of Sigmund Freud, I showed how his painstaking adherence to the psycho-analytical method of investigation gradually, indeed over the entire span of 45 years of work, led to serial revision of concepts of the development of personality. While his training and era disposed him to think in terms of energy (instincts) and their control or modification (vicissitudes), his discoveries with patients confronted him with evidence about structure and organisation. Psycho-analysis, as a theoretical branch of psychology, finally took its present form in 1923 when, with the publication of "The Ego and the Id", Freud gave specific significance to the term "meta-psychology" as the special province of psycho-analysis, examining the human personality from four viewpoints: its development (genetic aspect), its structure (earlier called the topographic aspect), its mechanisms of operation (dynamic aspect) and its disposition of psychic "energy" (economic aspect).

While in the previous Chapter we followed Freud's views of childhood sexuality through to the time of his death in 1939, we more or less stopped about 1911 as regards the evolution of his view on the structural aspect of personality development in children. Even in the 1905 edition of the "Three Essays on Sexuality" he recognised phases of erogenous-zone-primacy, the mouth, anus, genitals. But these were viewed as leading zones either in object relations (allo-erotic) or for auto-erotic gratification. His conception was that these zones, or fixation to them, served as foci of the crystallisation of the pathological conflicts which in adult life would give rise to neuroses and psychoses.

In 1913, in the paper "The Disposition of Obsessional Neurosis" he writes: "To begin with, I had only distinguished, first the phase of auto-erotism, during which the subject's component instincts, each on its own account" (*i.e.*, devoid of organisation) "seek for the satisfaction of their desires in his own body, and then the combination of all the component instincts for the choice of an object, under the primacy of the genitals acting on behalf of reproduction. The analysis of the paraphrenias" (paranoia and schizophrenia) "has, as

21

we know, necessitated the insertion between them of a stage of narcissism, during which the choice of an object has already taken place but that object coincides with the subject's own ego. And now we see the need for yet another stage to be inserted before the final shape is reached—a stage in which the component instincts have already come together for the choice of an object and that object is already something extraneous in contrast to the subject's own self, but in which *the primacy of the genital zone has not yet been established. The component instincts which dominate this pregenital organisation*" (*first use of this term*) "of sexual life are the anal-erotic and sadistic ones."[1]

Here the important shift has been made, from a preoccupation with instincts and their modes of operation in children to a primary concern with organisation of the psychic apparatus. Freud was also keenly aware that any such concept of phases of organisation would require also concepts of transitions both progressive and regressive. The possibility of a more advanced state would need to exist in the less advanced one. For instance, in this paper he notes the elementary structure of what later becomes the definitive bisexuality (XIII, 322), "We must not forget that the antithesis between male and female, which is introduced by the reproductive function, cannot be present as yet at the stage of pregenital object choice. We find in its place the antithesis between trends with an active and with a passive aim . . ."

By 1915, in the new edition of the *Three Essays* he added another pregenital organisation to his schema, having discovered it through the analysis of the processes of normal and pathological identification in character formation. "The first of these" (phases) "is the oral, or as it might be called, the cannibalistic pregenital organisation. Here sexual activity has not yet been separated from the ingestion of food; nor are opposite currents within the activity differentiated. The *object* of both activities is the same; the sexual *aim* consists in the incorporation of the object—the prototype of a process which, in the form of identification, is later to play such an important psychological part."[2]

The interest in character structure, in addition to the traditional concern with pathological symptoms, had already been stimulated by Freud in 1908 in a paper on "Character and Anal Erotism" (*S.E.*, IX) where he had described his famous triad of anal character traits, orderliness, parsimony and stubbornness. The researches, particularly by Freud, Karl Abrahams, Ernest Jones and Sándor

---

[1] Freud, "The Disposition to Obsessional Neurosis", *S.E.*, Vol. XII, p. 317.
[2] *Three Essays* . . ., *S.E.*, Vol. VII, p. 198.

Ferenczi, which filled the literature post World War I, brought under scrutiny the whole of human conduct. In one enlightening and amusing clinical paper after another, social behaviour, clothing, food habits, work habits, hobbies, entertainments—in short the whole galaxy of human eccentricity which forms our culture—were scrutinised for their infantile sources and their economic significance. By this means the child inside the man began to be revealed in a manner which not only altered the scope of psycho-analysis as a method of psychological research but also as a therapy. In addition its significance for education and child-rearing shone forth and the ground was laid for the first direct psycho-analytic work with children by Hermine von Hug-Hellmuth, Anna Freud and Melanie Klein.

From this period of intense preoccupation with the unconscious roots and the developmental basis of character, the most important type of advance, as regards psychosexual development, is to be found in the fact that one discovery after another clothed the conception of "pregenital organisation" with flesh and blood. Where Freud had erected the framework, Abraham filled in the details. In a relatively brief period of eight years following the end of World War I, prior to his premature death at the age of 48, he produced a series of papers, culminating in his famous "Short Study of the Development of the Libido" (1924) in which he organised findings derived from pioneer work with manic-depressive and schizophrenic patients. It is from this work that the entire line of new developments associated with the name of his student, Melanie Klein, have their source. These I plan to discuss in the fourth Chapter.

In substance what Karl Abraham contributed to our understanding of children's emotional and mental life and their personality development had elements both of elaboration and of a new integration. He concluded that the psychosexual basis of character had to be understood in relation both to *phases of erogenous zone primacy and stages of object-relation organisation.* Thus in his hands the earlier differentiation of three phases of development leading to the crisis of the Oedipus complex now appeared as six phases; (1) oral sucking, (2) oral biting or cannibalistic, (3) early anal or anal expulsive, (4) late anal or anal retentive, (5) early genital or phallic and (6) later genital phase.

In addition, Freud's divisions of the object-relation stages, namely auto-erotic, narissistic and allo-erotic (or object love), were expanded to account for the problem of ambivalence, *i.e.*, both love and hate toward an object, and the progression from part-objects to whole-objects in the child's experience and feelings. It can be recognised that the concept now of a stage of development, made up of both the phase of instinctual primacy and the stage of object relation, became a highly complicated affair, the description of which would involve a definitive answer to a number of specific questions as follows:

(1) what is the erogenous zone primacy? (oral, anal or genital)
(2) what is the object of this impulse? (whole person or a part of a person's body)
(3) what is the aim of this impulse? (to take in, to retain, to expel, to destroy, to fill, to empty, etc. These innumerable aims might be viewed all as variants of two, to take or to give)
(4) what is the quality of the impulse? (loving, destructive or ambivalent)
(5) what consequence is expected for the subject? (relief of pain, lessening of anxiety, gratification of desire, enhancement of development, etc.)
(6) what consequence is felt to befall the object?
(7) to what extent is the subject concerned with the fate of his object?

In order to make this as clear as possible, in a way that will facilitate the reading of the next Chapter on the developments since 1924, I will attempt to describe Abraham's scheme in my own words, for, unfortunately, he has not given us a summary. Since this is drawn together from his various papers, it may not be exact in detail. In regard to the duration of the different phases I can only guess his opinion.

I Early Oral Stage

At birth and for days or weeks thereafter, the baby exists as totally auto-erotic, its various zones experiencing distress or gratification in ignorance of any differentiation of self or object. The balance in the total experience of gratification *vs.* distress may determine the characterologic balance optimism-pessimism in later life. The mouth and its function of sucking is the leading zone and mode of activity. This is the probable point of fixation for regression to catatonia.

II Late Oral Stage

The baby is dominated by his mixture of love and hate toward the breast, which is not clearly recognised as an object in its own right but is devoured by biting (in phantasy) and either destroyed or established as a part of the self by identification, depending on the balance of love and hate. Since parts of the body are not clearly differentiated, breasts, penis, buttocks, eyes, cheeks, etc., are easily inter-changed and confused. Where narcissism is complete and destructiveness is intense and concern for the object nil, the fixation point for the development of schizophrenia takes shape. Where the cannibalism is more loving and the part of the self identified with the incorporated object more solicitously held, the fixation point for melancholia takes shape. This crisis is probably resolved at the time of weaning. Character balances involving greed, ambition, generosity, dependence and envy may have their roots here.

III Early Anal Sadistic Stage

The baby's preoccupation and leading zonal pleasure has moved to his anus, where his faeces are treated partly as an object that has been incorporated and partly as a product of this part of the body, which is felt to be very powerful and destructive. Objects in the outside world tend to be rewarded with idealised faeces or destroyed with omnipotent faeces in a highly ambivalent and unstable way. As a consequence attacks upon the anus by bad objects are intensely feared. The overestimation of the faeces as food makes a contribution to the pre-disposition to melancholia, while the power to expel objects from the anus contributes to the tendency to mania. Paranoia is very closely linked to the fear of persecution by bad objects getting into the anus. Consequently activity-passivity as a character balance may be determined by the interplay of these impulses and anxieties. Similarly attitudes toward work, productivity, examinations and truthfulness spring from these conflicts, which are probably aggravated by premature cleanliness training and greatly affected by the outcome of weaning.

IV Late Anal-Sadistic Stage

While the anus is the leading erogenous zone, it is the rectum or abdominal contents of self and objects which preoccupy the small child. The relations are still very ambivalent, but less concerned with the faeces as such than with what they are felt to contain that has been either created by the self or obtained from objects. Since external objects are less cannibalistically taken in but more felt as suppliers of substances, preoccupation with possessions and their retention is predominant over desire to emulate objects in behaviour or capacities. Where sadism is severe the fixation point is formed for the obsessional neurosis. Conflicts of this period, which extend generally to the age of two, serve as the focus for the adult character traits regarding material possessions, control over people and objects, obstinacy *vs.* docility.

V Early Genital or Phallic and
VI Late Genital Stage

Abraham's views more or less followed Freud's formulations, as given in Chapter 2. His emphasis would also have been on the

castration complex, the Oedipus conflict and the later development
of femininity. His specific contribution to the understanding of these
stages lies in his emphasis on the progression of object-love from
exclusive preoccupation with the genitals and from a high degree of
ambivalence toward resolution of ambivalence, with the emergence
of love for whole, unique, human objects. This advance he felt to be
essential for the later psychosexual organisation of the adult.

What sort of conception of a baby or a child is envisaged here?
One feels that such influence as the theory of evolution, archaeology
and the new science of anthropology contributed to an unconscious
model of development that was partly a confused mixture, partly a
layered structure, like the archaeologist's tor, or like the social
structure of a recently civilised primitive tribe, a microcosm of
evolution where cold-blooded impulses were being changed into
warm-blooded ones. Certainly the ideas of development and
regression implied that a stage might be successfully traversed but
was never truly dismantled. Rather, it is seen as remaining always
in existence in the unconscious, like a reserve military unit, ready to
be mobilised if stress should become excessive. On the other hand,
pathological symptoms or character traits seemed, in this scheme,
like recalcitrant members of the primitive tribe, who would not put
on clothes or secretly practised their pagan rites. As yet no clearly
defined "geography" of mental life had been elaborated, no "psychic
reality" peopled by infantile and child parts of the self and internal
objects had been formulated. Freud had already described the
conscience as a psychic "structure" related to the incorporation of
the parents, and Abraham had traced some of the pathological
consequences of incorporation of primitive objects in melancholia or
invasion by them in paranoia. But the outward orientation of all
normal mental life was held to contrast with supposedly abnormal
preoccupation with internal processes, as in the hypochondrias, and
the unconscious was still the region of irrationality. However, up to
this point the entire structure of psycho-analytic theory about
development had been drawn from the work with neurotic and
psychotic adults, unalloyed with the direct observation of children
in any systematic way.

In the next Chapter the changes in these views brought about by
the application of the psycho-analytic method directly to children
will become apparent. I mentioned that the great advances in
psycho-analysis in the 1920's produced a coherent theory of
personality-development and gained for this young science a new
interest among educators and other people concerned with child
rearing. Its earlier audience had been almost exclusively medical
since it seemed to deal with the origin of pathological nervous

symptoms only. This new, broadened interest also attracted new workers who aspired to make the benefits of psycho-analytical treatment available to children as well as adults.

What could be said, however, to be disappointing in the conception of child development which had evolved, say, by the time of Abraham's "Short Study" (1924) is that it semeed very little, if at all, to deal with children and their development in day to day life. One is unable to see the child for the theories, you might say. I think that it is in fact a correct representation of the state of affairs in the field of psycho-analysis up to the mid-1920's. By devoted, detailed and painstaking work with neurotic and psychotic adult patients, these pioneers of psycho-analysis had managed to construct a very abstract and diagrammatic "child", a psycho-analytic child, which bore the same resemblance to a human child that a world of adze-axes, potsherds and ritual figurines does, for instance, to the teeming life in an actual neolithic village. We cannot suspect those early workers of lack of imagination. On the contrary, it was necessary to curb ebullient imagination in favour of strict adherence to scientific evidence gained by the psycho-analytic method which Freud constantly urged upon his followers. No, it was the method itself which by its very nature could only reveal the unconscious relics of childhood organisations, not the child itself, just as it is only the relatively imperishable items of cultural bric-a-brac which come down to the archaeologist.

This was significantly changed by the three women, von Hug-Hellmuth, Anna Freud and Melanie Klein, who adapted the psycho-analytic method to children. But even here, with little children from two and a half years onward, the same reservation holds, for while we may now seem to have a vibrant and panoramic view of childhood development, the first years of life are still largely reconstruction, schematic. Direct observation of infants by psycho-analysts has begun to bring the baby to life. In the next Chapter I will describe how the therapeutic work with children, especially the discoveries of Melanie Klein, have now enabled us to see the child more completely in his internal world and extrenal relations, in his emotional and intellectual development, in his power as well as in his weakness, in his goodness and badness, innocence and corruption. But again a word of caution: this is the *child complete*-in-the-analytic-playroom. There remains a considerable work of transposition before one can utilise the findings of psycho-analysis to see the child-complete-in-the-classroom or in-the-home, for instance.

CHAPTER 4

From Pain-and-Fear to Love-and-Pain

In the three previous Chapters I have described first, the psycho-analytic method in its excellence and limitations. Next, I traced Freud's early discoveries about infantile sexuality and his theories about the development of children particularly in so far as it forms the background for pathological symptoms in adult life. In the third Chapter I outlined the sudden and unexpected development, largely due to the work of Freud and Abraham in the post World War I years. This transformed psycho-analysis from a method for investigating and treating nervous illness into a special branch of psychology, *meta-psychology*. A new, multi-dimensional and coherent conception of personality development took shape in terms of developmental phases and organisational series.

But I ended with a note of semi-apology for the living child who could not be found among the ponderous theories. I did however promise to remedy this defect by describing the developments between 1926 and 1946 which grew out of the direct analytic work with children, and especially the work of Melanie Klein with very young children.

Much of the impetus for this direct approach to the child had come from an unusal bit of work by Freud himself, reported in 1909 (*S.E.* X) and known to analysts as the case of "Little Hans". This little boy of five, suffering from a phobia of horses but generally a healthy, intelligent and normal child, was not treated by Freud but by the child's father, who was acquainted with the findings of psycho-analysis, under Freud's close supervision. The clinical result was highly satisfactory, but left Freud very doubtful that such a treatment could be accomplished by many parents or by an analyst directly. It was only the development of modified technique by the three women I have mentioned, the so-called "Play-Technique", that made the direct treatment of children by the rigorous application of the psycho-analytic method possible. While Anna Freud at first advocated only a partial application of the method as compared with the more meticulous use of the transference by Melanie Klein, over the past 30 years these technical differences have largely disappeared. The advances of theory which partly resulted from this work, along with discoveries from adults, now make it possible to bring the psycho-analytical method to bear with some degree of success on all personality disorders of children from age two onward.

The case of little Hans did much to reassure Freud and his circle that their reconstruction of the oedipal period and the so-called "infantile neurosis" which had been hypothecated as a precursor of the later adult neurosis—that this infantile edition of the disturbance did in fact exist. The case helped to infuse the theories of bisexuality and ambivalence with vitality, as a real little boy, struggling with his love and hatred of mother and father and with his own male and female genital desires, came to life in Freud's beautiful paper, probably the most delightful in the entire psycho-analytical literature. To Freud's power as a scientist was mated a rich literary genius which makes his works, either in the original German or in the faultless translations of James and Alix Strachey of the *Standard Edition*, truly part of the world's great literature.

Melanie Klein possessed no such literary gifts. The blunt, staccato and excessively condensed style of presentation of her early findings in *The Psychoanalysis of Children* (1932) did nothing to assuage the opposition to her ideas. While Little Hans had danced across Freud's page like a troubled little prince, poor Rita, Trude, Erna, Peter and others of the 18 cases cited by Melanie Klein emerge as grossly abnormal, monstrous in their preoccupations and frightening in their violence. The explanation is, of course, not literary alone, for indeed these children were seriously ill, already enmeshed in disturbances which could only have led to severe neurosis or psychosis in adult life. In addition, the very nature of their illness involved the more primitive, more violently ambivalent, more dehumanised part-object levels of their mental life concerned with their pregenital organisations. Consider an excerpt, for instance: "Trude, aged three and three-quarters, used repeatedly to pretend in her analysis that it was night-time and that we were both asleep. She then used to come softly over to me from the opposite corner of the room (which was supposed to be her own bedroom) and threaten me in various ways, such as that she was going to stab me in the throat, throw me out of the window, burn me up, take me to the police, etc. She would want to tie up my hands and feet, or she would lift up the rug on the sofa and say she was doing 'Po-Kaki-Kuki'. This, it turned out, meant that she wanted to look inside her mother's bottom for the 'Kakis' (faeces), which signified children to her. On another occasion she wanted to hit me in the stomach, and declared that she was taking out my 'A-as' (stool) and was making me poor. She then seized the cushions, which had repeatedly figured as children, and crouched down with them behind the sofa. There she exhibited every sign of fear, covered herself up, sucked her fingers and wetted herself. She used to repeat this whole process whenever she made an attack on me. It corresponded in every detail with the way she had behaved in bed when, at a time when she was not yet two, she had been overtaken by very severe night terrors. At that time, too, she had run into her parents' bedroom again and again at night without being able to say what it was she wanted. Analysis showed that her wetting and dirtying herself were attacks upon her parents copulating with each other, and in this way removed the symptom. Trude had wanted to rob her pregnant mother of her children, to kill her and to take her place in coitus with her father."[1]

This is an uncompromising presentation which runs counter to whatever may remain within us of the tendency to idealise children or to see childhood as innocent, happy. How different from Little Hans, whose manly desires growing out of admiration for his father, to be big, to have a big fine penis and to marry his beautiful mother tend to bring approving smiles and nods of encouragement from us.

Still, here in a case like Trude, was rich confirmation of Freud's and Abraham's theories about the infantile roots of obsessional neurosis, the anal-retentive stage, the part-object nature of the relationships in this highly ambivalent pregenital organisation. And as such, naturally these findings with young children were welcomed into the literature of psycho-analysis. But it can easily be seen that such findings contain more than mere confirmation of theories derived from adult work. They reveal the pain in the ill child and demand our attention. This imperative could not really stand side by side with the Dickensian idealisation of childhood which viewed suffering as coming only from the outside, to orphaned, ill, handicapped or neglected children. It demanded recognition that children do not emerge from a cocoon of bliss into the ordeal of school age, but are born into a bedlam of infantile anxieties, in the midst of which their only oasis is the physical presence of a beloved or at least trusted adult. Every area of their daily life—eating, sleeping, playing, urinating, defecating, learning, being bathed, dressed, or treated for physical ills—each was seen to be molested with anxieties of a type seen with adults only in the most severe mental disorders—the "psychotic anxieties" of persecution.

Freud had taken the view, derived from his work with adults, that the institution of conscience, which he called the "super-ego", developed as the "heir to the Oedipus complex", that is, that the resolution of this infantile conflict of love and hate took the form of the establishment of the parents, and particularly the parent of the

1 Melanie Klein, *The Psycho-analysis of Children*, London, Hogarth Press, 1932, p. 25.

same sex, as an internal figure which functioned as a conscience. His studies of disorders more serious than hysteria, such as obsessional neurosis, manic-depressive states and schizophrenia had shown him that they involved very severe disturbances of this structure, the super-ego, especially in the form of its being excessively harsh, even savagely murderous. But since these illnesses did not seem to appear until later childhood in the case of obsessions or adolescence in the case of schizophrenia, he concluded that the alterations of the super-ego occurred at these later times. He therefore saw no reason to modify his views about the time of origin of conscience, even though he recognised that the so-called "fixation point" of these illnesses lay in the pregenital phases of development, *i.e.*, prior to age three generally.

Consequently, the second significant modification of the picture of early childhood which came from Melanie Klein's work with young children was the recognition that the internal world of the child was already, or perhaps *especially*, at this early age highly complex, peopled in the child's conscious and unconscious phantasies by figures good and bad with whom it was in a constant state of conflict or alliance, ever shifting. Whether the many figures, linked in such important ways to the father, the mother and to various parts of their bodies, should be called collectively the "early super-ego" or merely "super-ego precursors" is not one of great importance today, but fierce battles raged over it in the years following Freud's death. The really important modification of our view of children was the growth of the rich concept of "psychic reality", which is by no means a mere euphemism to imply that children set great store by phantasy. It is a rigorous scientific concept which recognises that the growth of a child's mind takes place by a continually oscillating process, in which his activities with figures in the outside world modify the qualities of internal figures, in conscious and unconscious phantasy. Play, dreams, phantasy, masturbation and other types of auto-erotism, in turn affect these internal figures and thus alter the child's view of the outside world in respect of values and meaning.

Let us go back for a moment to Melanie Klein's description of Trude's play representation of her night terrors. These had taken shape at a time, around age two, when her mother was pregnant. Trude's masturbation phantasies, in which she robbed her internal mother of faeces, babies and riches changed her mother into a frightening persecutor. This internal situation caused her to have night terrors which were inconsolable because her trust in her external mother was interfered with by a view confused with her internal situation. This made her wet and soil herself, which in fact caused some difficulty with her mother in the outside world; this in turn increased Trude's envy and resentment, her tendency to masturbate, and so on.

A certain amount of disagreement still exists in psycho-analytic circles concerning the date of onset of these internal relations, the formation of this world of "psychic reality", for again Melanie Klein in her uncompromising fashion insisted that the evidence indicated that these processes commenced with the very beginning of post-natal life. The exact dating is of little consequence for our purposes here. What matters is the recognition of the immense importance to the child's mental and *physical* development of this interior world of the mind, peopled with a host of objects, good and bad, which only very slowly and incompletely are integrated to form the parental figures of Freud's "super-ego".

I wish to stress "good and bad" because this brings us to the third great modification of our image of children's mental life, derived from the work of Melanie Klein, in a way the most important from our point of view here, of bringing the child to life amongst the theories. In the eleven year period bridging World War II, 1935 to 1946, in four monumental papers she formulated what are known as the concepts of the *paranoid-schizoid* and *depressive positions* in object relations, which, to my mind, have brought psycho-analysis into the most intimate relation to the pulse of life, the drama of love and hatred, good and evil, creation and destruction, growth and decay, beauty and ugliness, sanity and madness in individuals and in societies. The presentation of these concepts forms the finale, the coda of these historical Chapters and requires a certain poetic flight to capture their beauty.

From her work with young children, and later with very ill adults, Melanie Klein concluded that the war between love and hate and between good and evil commences at birth or shortly thereafter—that the pain and fear, and the rage which accompanies them, threaten the infant's desire to live to an extent which is a serious threat to its ability, in fact, to survive. If it is to survive in a reasonably healthy way, it must deal with this terrible state by a mechanism called splitting, whereby it divides itself and its objects most severely into idealised "good" and persecuting "bad" segments. The idealised "good" parts of the self attempt to ally themselves with idealised "good" objects, in the first instance with the feeding breast of the mother, or its representative. These are internal processes. A fundamental alliance, the mother-child idealised, forms the prototype for the development of love, trust, gratitude and hope.

But this alliance, the idealised relationship, is threatened from all sides, both internally and externally. Every pain, disappointment or shock attacks the trust in the goodness and strength of the object. Every separation brings loneliness, jealousy which attacks gratitude. Envy of the goodness, beauty, strength or competence of the object works against the love. Any sign of wear, weakness or aging under- mines the hope.

What I have described so far is the paranoid-schizoid position, in which all safety against persecution, pain and death is felt to derive from the strength and services of these idealised objects, at first the mother's breast, then a more coherent concept of the mother, later the father as well, and so on. But the accent is on *being protected from pain and danger*. In this organisation of the personality the good objects are valued, even loved or worshipped, but for their services—in a word, selfishly. At its best this orientation achieves an enlightened self-interest, akin to the benevolent despot's attitude to his subjects. It cannot experience *concern*.

Where this primary splitting and idealisation of infant self and objects has satisfactorily taken place, where the parental services are reasonably adequate, where neither jealousy, envy nor intolerance to mental and physical pain are excessive, a miraculous and beautiful thing tends to take place, known in flat scientific jargon as the "phenomenology of the threshold of the depressive position". In the language of life, tender concern for the welfare of the beloved object tends to supersede selfish concern for the comfort and safety of the self. The capacity for sacrifice emerges—babies wait for their feeds instead of screaming, leave off sucking when more is still available in breast or bottle, try to control their sphincters to spare the mother, bear separation despite worry. Out of obedience, good- ness emerges; out of competitiveness, the capacity to work; out of toleration of deprivation, pride in development.

The beauty of these concepts helps us to see how children struggle, to comprehend their failures and their need to try again and again. At every juncture of a child's life he is presented with the dual problem of renouncing old services and developing new skills. At every juncture he must decide again whether to go forward or not, and, if forward, for what reason, enlightened self interest, fear, competitiveness—or concern for his good objects. Note that these concepts do *not* supersede the developmental stages and phases of organisation discovered by Freud and Abraham. Rather they explore the method of transition from phase to phase, and why at times development fails, how one failure increases the likelihood of the next, etc. These concepts are therefore primarily economic concepts, although we no longer think of "psychic energy" as an analogue of physical energy. They are "economic" not in a narrowly quantitative sense but more in the sense that a government may be said to have an *economic policy*. The economics of the self in relation to internal objects is governed in this way.[1]

The child's struggle to preserve his relations to his love objects, both internal and external, involves him in problems that bring into focus the attributes of courage, for time and time again the child will fail to preserve good faith at the level of the depressive position and will be faced with the pains of guilt, remorse, unworthiness, shame. Time and again his love will bring in its wake increments of powerful worry, loneliness, and jealousy during separation. When we understand how dearly little children must pay for their love relations in the face of their limited self-control, it helps us to be patient, to support them with resolution, to protect them from undue hardships or temptations. These concepts show us as adults the need to exemplify in our behaviour if we can qualities like courage, integrity and capacity for sacrifice which can be assimilated to strengthen the goodness of the child's internal objects upon whom they must, during separation and eventually, totally, depend for support.

Here then, these three developments, the revelation of early psychotic anxieties, the establishment of the overriding importance for development of "psychic reality" and the delineation of the economic concepts of paranoid-schizoid and depressive positions, are the discoveries of Melanie Klein, from 1921 to 1946, which have so greatly altered our understanding of the minds of children, and thereby changed so radically our judgment of the meaning of their behaviour.

---

[1] Space does not permit a full discussion of the relation of the various economic principles—repetition compulsion, pleasure-pain-reality principle and paranoid-schizoid-depressive positions—to one another.

SECTION B

ON FREUD'S THEORY OF
SEXUAL PSYCHOPATHOLOGY*

* Read to 2nd year students,"Institute of Psycho-analysis", London, 1968-69.

CHAPTER 5

The Clinical Phenomenology of Narcissism[1]

THE sources of information at our disposal—published works, letters, biography, society minutes, autobiographies and memoirs— do not, of course, separate out from the life of Freud the particular thread of his investigations of clinical psychopathology nor do the particular papers given in reference lend themselves to classification as "clinical". Yet this is a very distinct category of Freud's scientific work and an area of relation and interaction with colleagues. Surely in the period we are studying, embracing the later World War I period and its aftermath, the problems of the organisation, development and preservation of psycho-analysis as a scientific discipline and as a "movement" (whatever that means) occupied—or even overshadowed—much of his thought, as it found its way into print. Particularly the conflicts with Adler and later Jung dominate such papers as "The History of the Psycho-analytic Movement" and the "Wolf-Man" case history.

Jones relates how, to relieve Freud of some of this burden, the "Committee" was formed in 1912, but the disruption of communication during the war, not to mention Freud's own nationalistic enthusiasm at its start and despair toward its finish, probably prevented this group's protective mission from realisation.

On the other hand, the scarcity of patients during the war gave Freud an abundance of time for writing, to which we owe the long "Wolf-man" case history, the papers on meta-psychology and the first Introductory Lectures. Furthermore, taking "On Narcissism" as the opening gun in the salvo culminating in "The Ego and the Id", we can assume that the stocktaking period of the war made possible the immense productivity which gave us the Structural Theory (1920–26).

Nonetheless, it must be viewed as a period of reassessment rather than one of clinical discovery. Very likely after the war, being now a renowned figure and the leader of a scientific movement, Freud's cases tended to be of less psychopathological interest as his time was more and more taken up with students. For instance we know that

[1] It is necessary, for full comprehension of the next two Chapters, that the reader be familiar with the content of those of Freud's works to which reference is made, a list of which can be found at the end of each Chapter.

he more or less supported the "Wolf-man" in his post-war poverty, yet had to ask Ruth Mack Brunswick to undertake his further treatment when the patient had his paranoid breakdown in 1926. The clinical work by Freud had, of course, been done before the war. The only case history we have from the post-war era is the case of female homosexuality, which was a brief and unsuccessful attempt at therapy with an 18 year old girl. Although cases are discussed in other papers, six in "A Child is Being Beaten", two in "Jealousy, Paranoia and Homosexuality" for instance, we cannot really see the psycho-analyst Freud at work. Consequently, the case of the homosexual adolescent girl is of special interest, for we are able to juxtapose it to Freud's work with "Dora", thus gaining a vantage point for estimating the changes in technique and consequent changes in data which 20 years of practice had brought about.

One other historical perspective should perhaps be kept in mind in pursuing this thread of Freud's interest in the phenomenology of narcissism, namely the situations of mourning in his own life. The self-analysis and the work with Dora seem to have an intimate connection with the death of Freud's father. Between 1914 and 1923 he lost his half-brother Emmanuel, his daughter Sophie (1920), and his grandson Heins (1923). His mother lived until 1930. We have reason to think that mourning took Freud very painfully and that when he writes (*S.E.* 14, p. 244) that the libido must be detached from "each single one of the memories and expectations" related to the lost love object, he is talking from first hand experience. One can see that he was a bit shocked at the callousness with which the "Wolf-man" had greeted his sister's suicide with conscious satisfaction at now being the sole heir. Freud was prone to see the subsequent weeping at Pushkin's grave as a displacement of his grief for the sister, on the grounds of her unfulfilled literary gifts. It seems far more likely that he was narcissistically identified with his sister in this outburst and that it was linked to the solicitude for his ill father which had produced the breathing-compulsion and the pity for aged and crippled men in his latency period.

But of course this was one of the hazards of the entire approach of that case history, with its emphasis on reconstruction and its aim of refuting Jung and Adler. In the immediate clinical situation Freud clearly had a very keen eye for genuine grief, with its loss of interest in a world now impoverished, its pain of relinquishment, its struggle against resentment as of a desertion. Melancholia he could recognise as basically painless, but rather provocative of pain in all those concerned with the patient as he arrogantly proclaims his sinfulness, monumental unworthiness and saintly self-abasement (pp. 246–48).

It seems that the key to the progress in clinical psychopathology during this period of Freud's work resides just here, in his having made a fundamental distinction in "On Narcissism" between object-choice according to the narcissistic (p. 89—what he is, was, wishes to be or once was in part) or the anaclitic (the woman who feeds, the man who protects) type. He was in a position to work out the clinical details in three different directions: the structural direction, eventuating in "The Ego and the Id" with the evolution from ideal ego (On Narcissism) to ego ideal (Mourning and Melancholia) to superego (Ego and Id); secondly in the topographic (later structural) and dynamic areas which seemed to Freud to govern the differentiation of neurosis from psychosis; and finally in the area of character, manifestations of the effects of identification on the one hand and sublimations on the other.

It probably does not matter to us very greatly, in our approach to the clinical problems, that Freud moved, over this ten year period, from the preoccupation with disposition of the libido (object-libido and narcissistic libido) and the topographic concern with conscious, preconscious and unconscious (word-representation *vs.* thing-representation) onto the structural level of formulation (locus of conflict: ego-id in neurosis; ego-external world in psychosis, and ego-superego in the so-called "narcissistic psycho-neuroses"). What seems important was the process whereby new observations (such as those on the disposition of the libido in organic disease, hypochondria and erotic life) led to new concepts (narcissism) and new concepts led to new observations (the differentiation of mourning and melancholia) which led to new concepts (super-ego, eventually) which led to new observations (on homosexuality, perversions, fetishisms). The history of the era is in this regard a perfect example of how Freud worked in both deductive and inductive ways.

Through this time of change in emphasis from libido theory to structural theory, certain concepts became much stronger in their clinical reference, particularly fixation, regression and ambivalence. These three are very greatly emphasised in the "Wolf-man" case history—for instance the little boy's fixation to passive aims as a result of his sister's seduction of him (age three and a half), or his regression to anality in the formation of his obsessional illness that overcame the phobia and naughtiness (age four and a half), or the masculine and feminine ambivalence to his father which made of him the object hidden in the wolf-phobia. All that is seen in libido-theory terms.

If we turn to the clinical discussion in "Jealousy, Paranoia and Homosexuality" (1922) we find the concept of fixation stated mainly in terms of object (*e.g.*—mother-fixated), ambivalence in terms of affects (reversibility of love and hate in paranoia) and regression in terms of identification (regression to an identification with the mother in the homosexual male) rather than of stages of the development of the libido. This carries an important lesson, which not only justifies a primarily historical approach to the teaching of psychoanalysis, but defines it as the only means of showing how history takes place in our science. There is no purpose to be served by searching for "definitive" concepts, "correct" theories, "modern" outlooks, etc. The truth of the matter—and it is just as true in other sciences though it may be less apparent—theories are only tools for handling observations already made (notational function) and for formulating new investigations (hypothetical function).

To summarise, I have tried to show you the clinical trail that Freud was following—from general observations of love and parenthood, to the specific psychopathological phenomena such as melancholia, homosexuality, hypochondria—utilising the new concept of narcissism as his probe. I have also tried to make clear the reorganisation of theory which followed, and in the next Chapter I will try to show how this new theory brought into prominence the phenomenon of masochism and opened up to investigation the whole area of the perversions. At that point we will be able to see how the older concepts of ambivalence, fixation and regression, mating with newer ones of identification (and even an incipient concept of splitting of the ego) began to carry Freud's clinical work in directions which illness and age did not allow him to follow to completion.

REFERENCES

"From the History of an Infantile Neurosis", *S.E.*, 17, 1917.

"On Narcissism", *S.E.*, 14, 1914.

"Mourning and Melancholia", *S.E.*, 14, 1917.

"Psychogenesis of a Case of Homosexuality in a Woman", *S.E.*, 18, 1920.

"Some Neurotic Mechanisms in Jealousy, Paranoia and Homosexuality", *S.E.*, 18, 1922.

"Neurosis and Psychosis", *S.E.*, 19, 1924.

CHAPTER 6

Clinical Approach to the Perversions

In the previous Chapter I attempted to show one current of advance in Freud's grapplings with problems of clinical psychopathology during the decade 1917–27 (expressed in terms, of course, of publication dates). We can generally assume a considerable lag between writing and publication early in this period, for instance the "Wolf-man" history was written in 1914 but published in 1918 and is therefore really more contemporaneous with "On Narcissism" than with "A Child is Being Beaten". And yet the papers of the post-war period which I wish to discuss seem to hark back to the clinical experience of the "Wolf-man" very often, although not explicitly stated. But that this case made a great impression upon Freud cannot be doubted, for as late as 1937 he was still referring to it.

The whole line of papers from "A Child is Being Beaten" (1919) through "The Economic Problem of Masochism" (1924) to the paper on "Fetishism" (1927) seems to have been inspired by the work with the "Wolf-man". It is well to remember that the patient lived in Vienna after the war and had his paranoid breakdown there in 1926. What I propose to try to demonstrate is that Freud took hold of the concept of masochism very firmly in relation to the clinical phenomena of the case itself but kept losing it in later years during the transition in his notational system from the libido theory to the structural theory.

Freud goes to great length to plead the theory of the primal scene in Section IV on the wolf-dream, only to beg the entire question later in Section VIII (p. 97), "All that we find in the prehistory of neurosis is that a child catches hold of this phylogenetic experience where his own experience fails him"—*i.e.*, threats, seduction or exposure to parental coitus. In another paper written about the same time ("A Case of Paranoia Running Counter to the Theory of the Disease", *S.E.*, 14, 1915) he uses the theory of the primal scene to great advantage in explaining the woman patient's delusion that her relation with her lover had been overheard or even photographed: "The patient's lover was still her father, but she herself had taken her mother's place. The part of the listener had then to be allotted to a third person".

I cite these two references as the core of the case I wish to present, namely that the situation of the primal scene as laid out in the "Wolf-man's" dream was the key phantasy (or historical fact) in the material of sexual deviates of all sorts upon which Freud was building a great addendum to the "Three Essays on Sexuality", never really gathered together, even in the "New Introductory Lectures".

Let us pursue it further. From what he calls "The Primal Period" Freud traces the following events: the primal scene (during which the baby interrupted the parental coitus by passing a stool); the early eating difficulties brought to an end by the implied danger of death; the early scene with "Grusha" (meaning "pear" in Russian) and its link with enuresis, fire dreams, the butterfly phobia and the later falling in love with servant girls. These form the background of the "Wolf-man's" active and later masculine strivings as well as his tendencies to regression to oral sadism (cannibalism). On the other hand Freud traces the theme of the "Wolf-man's" passivity and its ramifications into his femininity, on the one hand, and his masochism on the other, to the baby's passage of the stool at the primal scene and his later bowel difficulties which were related to his mother's gynaecological troubles. Thus the complaint of impaired sense of reality, relieved only by enemata, is traced to the theme of having been "born with a caul", the narcissistic expectation of eternal good fortune (shattered by gonorrhoea) and his little boy's cruelty to small animals representing the mother's internal babies.

This latter passive current of potential anal (vaginal) femininity was altered to passive masculinity (phallic) by his sister's seduction and her tales about Nanya.

From the tracing and reconstruction of this primal scene and its two dominant currents of excitement Freud draws two astonishing conclusions:

(p. 101) ". . . he wishes he could be back in the womb, not simply in order that he might be reborn, but in order that he might be copulated with there by his father . . .";

(p. 102) "There is a wish to be back in a situation in which one was in the mother's genitals; and in this connection the man is identifying himself with his own penis . . .".

One need only combine these two statements to gain a third implication, namely that in coitus a man may be identified with his own penis as if it were a child inside the mother's genital being there copulated with by the father.

Now we may move on to the theme of the little boy's masochistic wish to be beaten on the penis and compare it with the formulation in "A Child is Being Beaten". (p. 189) "This being beaten is now a convergence of the sense of guilt and sexual love. It is not only the punishment for the forbidden genital relation, but also the regressive substitute for that relation".

Thus the little wolf-man's phantasies of "the heir to the throne being beaten on the penis" expressed both his guilt for his active masculine oedipal strivings and the secret satisfaction of his repressed passive feminine ones and drew him into a narcissistic identification with his mother suffering from menorrhagia, as in her statement to her doctor that she "could not go on living like this".

Unfortunately the "in the womb" aspect of the masculine and feminine phantasy seems to have got lost between 1914 and 1919, but when Freud returns to the theme again in 1924 in "The Economic Problem of Masochism" he is attempting to relate the problem to the duality of instinct proposed in "Beyond the Pleasure Principle". Accordingly that portion of the Death Instinct which is not directed outward as sadism is seen to be retained as a primary (1°) erotogenic masochism from which two developmental forms, feminine and moral masochism develop, while the "reintrojection" of projected destructiveness can produce a secondary (2°) masochism. This latter can effect a masochistic solution to any "developmental coating" and its associated anxiety, whether it be the fear of being eaten, beaten, castrated or copulated. These conclusions can be recognised to link with an earlier paper on character ("Some Character Types met with in Psycho-analytic Treatment"—*S.E.*, 14, 1916) where Freud had described "those wrecked by success", "criminals from a sense of guilt" and "The exceptions", all three aspects being recognisable in the character of the "wolf-man".

But of even more importance for our consideration here is the category of "feminine masochism", by which Freud meant the "normal" feminine attitude to sexuality in women, or, strangely, the perversion of masochism in men who phantasy or arrange in fact to be tied up, beaten, defiled, abused, etc. (p. 162) "The obvious interpretation, and one easily arrived at, is that the masochist wants to be treated like a small and helpless child, but particularly like a naughty child." But psycho-analytic study reveals the underlying feminine wish "of being castrated, or copulated with, or giving birth to a baby".

Thus the new "notation" of life and death instincts had offered Freud a way of dissecting the phenomenology of masochism into "feminine" and "moral", thus separating those factors related to guilt (moral) from those related to bisexuality (feminene erotogenic masochism in men and women) and also from those developmental forms of masochism (2°) resulting from defensive processes.

Again what I wish to stress is the interplay between deductive and inductive method in the progress of Freud's thinking. What had been an incidental aspect of the "Wolf-man's" reconstructed childhood could now be re-evaluated in the light of a new notation for instinct and psychic structure and used to explore similar aspects of other cases, giving promise of a new theory of the perversions. The projecting and reintrojecting of sadism, the kaleidoscopic shifting of identifications, the flux of bisexuality and the confusion of active-passive aims with masculine-feminine ones of a later developmental level could all begin to be correlated with each other. And the key was clearly the situation of the small child in relation to the primal scene or the primal phantasy.

It was only a short step now to solve the riddle of the fetish (On Fetishism—*S.E.*, 21, 1927) as combining the denial of castration anxiety (the phantasy that the woman does have a penis) and denial of the wish for castration. For again the new structural notation enabled Freud to state that contrary situations could exist side by side in the unconscious by the agency of a "split". This idea had been touched on at various points from the time of the "Project" but had only begun to be given real meaning earlier in the 1924 paper on "Neurosis and Psychosis", and would be amplified later in "Splitting of the Ego in the Process of Defence" (1937) and the "Outline" (1938). The way in which Freud states it in the 1924 paper is particularly germane to the struggles of the "Wolf-man." He says (pp. 152–53), "The thesis that neuroses and psychoses originate in the ego's conflicts with its various ruling agencies—that is, therefore, that they reflect a failure in the functioning of the ego, which is at pains to reconcile all the various demands made on it—this thesis needs to be supplemented in one further point. One would like to know in what circumstances and by what means the ego can succeed in emerging from such conflicts, which are certainly always present, without falling ill. This is a new field of research, in which no doubt the most varied factors will come up for examination. Two of them, however, can be stressed at once. In the first place, the outcome of all such situations will undoubtedly depend on economic considerations —on the relative magnitudes of the trends which are struggling with one another; in the second place, it will be possible for the ego to avoid a rupture in any direction by deforming itself, by submitting to encroachments on its own unity and even perhaps effecting a cleavage or division of itself. In this way the inconsistencies, eccentricities and follies of men would appear in a similar light to their sexual perversions, through the acceptance of which they spare themselves repression."

Thus Freud had come some considerable distance from the facile formula that neuroses were the negative of perversions. The complexity of the perversion and its relation to character had been opened up.

REFERENCES

"A Child is Being Beaten", *S.E.*, 17, 1919.
"Economic Problem of Masochism", *S.E.*, 19, 1924.
"On Fetishism", *S.E.*, 21, 1927.
"From the History of an Infantile Neurosis", *S.E.*, 18, 1918; Brunswick, R.M., I.J. Psa., 9;439, 1928. Gardiner, M. Publ. Phila. Psa., 2:32, 1952.

Part II

STRUCTURAL REVISION OF SEXUAL THEORY

INTRODUCTION TO PART II

PART I was not a history of psychoanalysis but a personal statement of a point of view about this history as background to what is now to follow. Part II is entirely made up of original contributions and the systematic tracing of their implications, in the light of Kleinian developments, for a revision of Sexual Theory. It will assume in the reader an intimate knowledge of psychoanalysis and its literature, and particularly of the work of Melanie Klein, Wilfred Bion, Herbert Rosenfeld, Hanna Segal and the author.

While most Chapters of Part II contain extensive clinical exemplification of the theory described, a reading of "The Psycho-analytical Process" (Heinemann 1967) is probably essential to a full appreciation.

Those Chapters which have previously been published separately, namely Chapters 7, 9, 14, 15 and 20, have been left in their original form.

SECTION A

PSYCHOSEXUAL DEVELOPMENT

CHAPTER 7

Identification and Socialisation in Adolescence[1]

SURELY, it will be said—and rightly—the analytic consulting room, in its heat of infantile intimacy, is not the place to study the social behaviour of adolescents. But it can, through clarification of the internal processes—of motivation and expectation, identification and alienation—throw a special and unparalleled light upon social processes to aid the sociologist, educator, psychiatrist, and all those persons of the adult community whose task it is to preserve the boundaries of the adolescent world and foster the growth and development of those still held within its vortex.

Our times reveal more clearly than other historical periods the truth of the existence of an "adolescent world" as a social structure, the inhabitants of which are the happy-unhappy multitude caught betwixt the "unsettling" of their latency period and the "settling" into adult life, the perimeter of which may not unreasonably be defined, from the descriptive point of view, as the establishment of mating and child rearing. From the metapsychological point of view of psycho-analysis, stripped as it is of social and moral evaluation, this passage from latency to adulthood may be described most forcefully in structural terms, whose social implications this chapter is intended to suggest.

The developmental pathways which traverse this world of adolescence lead from splitting in the self to integration, in relation to objects which, also by integration, are transformed from a multitude of part-objects to a family of whole objects in the internal world. Upon this model the external relationships *must* be regulated. As long as splitting of self and objects is still considerable, the experience of self will be highly fluctuating, depending on the dominance of one or other of the three types of psychic experience of identity in consciousness (described below). In a sense one may say that the *centre of gravity* of the experience of identity shifts—and in the adolescent it shifts wildly and continually.

This phenomenon, the continual shifting of the centre of gravity of the sense of identity, produces the characteristic quality of emotional instability seen in adolescence and since it is based on the underlying splitting processes, the varying states of mind are in very little

[1] Published in *Contemporary Psychoanalysis*, 3:96, 1967.

contact with one another. Hence the adolescent's gross incapacity to fulfil commitments to others, to carry through resolutions of his own or to comprehend why he cannot be entrusted with responsibilities of an adult nature. He cannot fully experience that the person who did not fulfil and the person who undertook to fulfil the commitment were the same person, namely himself. He therefore feels a continual grievance of the "brother's keeper" type.

His solution to this terrible state is a flight into group life where the various parts of himself can be externalised into the various members of the "gang". His own role becomes simplified greatly, though not completely, for status and function in the group is in flux to a certain extent. This flight-to-the-group phenomenon is equally evident dynamically in the adolescent who is not apparently a member of any gang, for, by being the "pariah", he fulfils a role which the gang formation requires, that of the totally alienated psychotic part of the personality in relation to those who are integrated in the gang. The isolate in turn projects his own more healthy parts.

I would remind you that this is not a descriptive definition of an age group but a metapsychological description of personality organisation typical of this age group, for we may meet "latency" in a fifty-year-old and "adolescence" at nine, structurally. The most important fact to be kept in mind in the following discussion is the transition from excessive and rigid splitting in latency, through the fluidity of adolescence in that matrix of personality where the more orderly and resilient splitting and differentiation of adult personality organisation must eventually be fashioned in order for the sense of identity to be established without rigidity.

The *experience of identity* is complex in structure and various in quality. Its unconscious basis we express by the concept of "identification", on the one hand, and the experience of "self", on the other. It contains both characterological and body-image facets and must be taken, in toto, as a summation of momentary states of mind, an abstraction of highly variable integration—from individual to individual—from moment to moment. The *experience of identity* also cannot exist in isolation, but only as foreground to the world of objects, internal and external—and to the laws of psychic and external reality.

There are three types of experiences which carry the feeling of identity, the experience of a part of the self, of identification with an object by introjection, and of identification with an object by projection. Each of the three has a very distinctive quality. The experience of a part of the self carries a feeling of limitation akin to littleness, tinged with loneliness. Introjective identification contains an aspirational element, tinged with anxiety and self-doubt. But the state of mind achieved by projective identification is fairly delusional in its quality of completeness and uniqueness. The attendant anxieties, largely claustrophic and persecutory, are held very separately in the mind from the identity experience.

I wish to come back now to the more central problem, the underlying severe confusion at all levels with which the adolescent is contending. As I have said, with the breakdown of the obsessional, rigid, and exaggerated splitting characteristic of latency structure, an uncertainty in regard to the differentiations, internal-external, adult-infantile, good-bad, and male-female which was characteristic of the pre-oedipal development reappears. In addition, perverse tendencies due to confusion of erogenous zones, compounded with confusion between sexual love and sadism, take the field. This is all "in order", as it were; the group life presents a modulating environment *vis-à-vis* the adult world and distinct from the child-world, well-equipped to bring this seething flux gradually into a more crystallised state—if the more psychotic type of confusion of identity due to massive projective identification does not play too great a role. To illustrate this I will describe two cases briefly.

But first to clarify the concept. Where the reappearance of masturbation brings with it a strong tendency, driven by infantile oral envy, to abandon the self and seize an object's identity by intrusion into it, the stage is set for a type of confusional anxiety which all adolescents experience to some extent. This confusion centres on their bodies and appears with the first pubic hair, the first breast growth, first ejaculation, and so forth. Whose body is it? In other words, they cannot distinguish with certainty their adolescent state from infantile delusions-of-adulthood induced by masturbation with attendant projective identification into internal objects. This is what lies behind the adolescent's slavish concern about clothes, make-up and hair-style, hardly less in the boys than in the girls.

Where this mechanism is very strongly operative and especially where it is socially "successful", the building up of the "false self", of which Winnicott has spoken, takes place.

Case Material

Rodney entered analysis at 18 after the complete academic failure of his first year at university. He was, two years later, able to regain a place and continue his education, but scholastic failure had promptly appeared in the analysis as the least of his difficulties. His latency period had been built on a severe split in his family adjustment, as he had been a devoted, endlessly helpful and unfailingly polite son among the otherwise rather stormy children. In fact, in his own eyes, he was never a child but a father-surrogate in all matters other than sexuality. To compensate, he appropriated as his due an absolute privacy and self-containment which, with the onset of puberty, became converted into a cover of absolute secrecy for a florid, delinquent bisexual life, while his family behaviour remained unchanged—now he was a "manly chap" instead of a "manly little chap".

In dividing himself among his gang he retained as his "self" the worst, most envious and cynical bit of himself. Consequently his relation to others tended to be both forceful and corrupting. The best parts of himself tended to remain projected into younger siblings, from whom he maintained a severe, protective distance.

More delusional states of identity occurred relatively infrequently and only under special circumstances—if he were driving his mother's car, or entertaining friends in an outbuilding he had been given as a study. These states could be dangerous indeed, physically and morally, but were soon recognised in the analysis and could be avoided. The re-establishment of contact with good parts, in a therapeutic alliance with the analyst and with internal objects, could take place. Progress was steady and rewarding.

Paul, on the other hand, had entered analysis in pre-puberty because of severe character restriction, with obsessional symptoms, nocturnal rituals, obvious effeminacy—all of which had existed for years but had been worsened by the break-up of the parents' marriage. The first period of analysis with another analyst utilising play technique had been virtually non-verbal. In those sessions he had been preoccupied with painting and art, producing a few pictures analysable in content but mainly endless preparations-for-painting consisting of mixing colours, making colour charts—in fact, concretely being daddy's artist-penis preparing the semen for the coming intercourse. As his symptoms had lessened and his school adjustment and work had improved, he broke off the analysis, returning to it only three years later when, after passing his O-levels and working his way to the position of vice-captain of his school, he found himself confronted with A-levels for which he was totally unprepared.

What had happened in the intervening time was that the building up of the school-self of athlete-artist-vice-captain had become totally time-consuming. It had to be compensated for by a gradual retrenchment from all academic subjects requiring thought or exact knowledge, in favour of those which he felt required talent or were based on vague statistics. He had become unable to study and at home or in school consumed his time in the busy-work of preparations or in the postures of absorption. His paranoia, particularly in relation to laughter, had to be hidden and his own mocking laugh, irreproachably tolerant in timbre, kept a steady stream of projection of feelings of humiliation penetrating into others.

Analytic work to gather together the infantile parts of himself into the transference and to differentiate the delusions-of-adulthood from his true adult personality was most tedious uphill work. Every separation brought a renewed flight by projective identification, represented in dreams by intruding into gardens, climbing into houses, leaving the main road for a trackless swamp, and so forth. For instance, in a Thursday session he had experienced a reawakening of gratitude toward his mother for providing the analysis, along with guilt about the motor scooter he had insisted on having and the hours of analysis he had missed or wasted. It had been his unusually strong reaction to the analysis of a dream which showed clearly that the preponderance of his infantile parts wanted analysis, not masturbation. In the dream *the crowd at a school dance was sitting at tables demanding food rather than going into the ballroom to* "*twist*". By Friday, however, he could whip himself into a state of arrogant contempt for the analysis because the analyst did not realise that Paul had now finally emerged from the chrysalis of "student". His art teacher on the other hand had said that his new picture was the first to show a style of his own rather than mimicry of others' styles. Relentlessly, then, he would spend the week-end mixing paints.

Paul presented a façade of social integration—the school captain— while Rodney seemed delinquent, corrupted, and isolated from society. But in fact, closer scrutiny shows that Rodney had a gang in which his identity was disseminated and from which it could be retrieved, while Paul had only "friends" who were his enforced colleagues while he was vice-captain and later captain of the school. In fact he was isolated—"well-liked"—to use the immortal phrase of Willy Loman in Arthur Miller's "Death of a Salesman".

These two cases are intended to show the important role of the group as a social pattern in adolescence, indicating that, no matter how delinquent or anti-social it may appear *vis-à-vis* the adult world, it is a holding position in relation to the splitting processes. By means of the dissemination of parts of the self into members of the group, amelioration of the masturbatory urge is achieved and social processes are set in train which foster the gradual lessening of the splitting, diminution of the omnipotence and easing of persecutory anxiety through achievement in the real world.

We must, however, turn back to our analytic experience at the other pole of the adolescent process to comprehend the basis of this dissemination. Experience in carrying latency children into puberty during analysis reveals this in a brilliant way which I will describe by means of a third case:

Juliet had come to analysis at the age of seven for deeply schizoid character difficulties which rendered her doll-like in appearance and demeanour, utterly submissive to excellent but highly idealised parents. This façade was fissured in two areas, explosion of faecal smearing on rare occasions and a witch-like hegemony over a younger sister and her little friends.

Six years of the most arduous analytic work broke through this, enabling her true femininity, artistic talents, and rich imagination to emerge by the time of her menarche. But her masculinity formed the basis of her social adaptation to peers, as shown by the formation of a gang of five girls, all intelligent, attractive, and athletic, who became the "trouble-makers" of her girls' school. The general pattern of a very revealing dream of that time was subsequently repeated, again and again. She seemed in the dream, *to be one of five convict men who were confined in a flimsy structure made of slats at the top of a tall tree. But every night they escaped and prowled about the village, returning unbeknown to their captors before dawn.*

This dream could be related to earlier material regarding masturbatory habits in which her fingers, in bed at night, explored the surfaces and orifices of her body, often accompanied by conscious adventuresome phantasies.

Two years later, when her femininity had established itself in the social sphere as well, she attended her first unchaperoned party, where the boys were somewhat older; drinking occurred, and sexual behaviour became rather open. To her surprise she behaved with a coolness and provocativeness which earned her the shouted epithet of "frigid tart" from a boy whose attempt to feel under her skirt she had skilfully repulsed.

That night she dreamed *that five convicts were confined to a wooden shed from which they were released by a bad squire on condition that they would steal fruit from the women with fruit stalls in the village and bring the loot to him.*

Here one can see that the delinquent organisation of the masculine masturbating fingers had been projected into the boys of the party by her "frigid tart" behaviour. The fact that the phantasies acted out were infantile and pregenital (anal and oral) was clearly indicated by the stealing of food, from the bottom, a theme well known from the earlier years of analytic work.

This masturbatory theme, the personification of the fingers, seems in fact to turn up with extraordinary frequency in our analytic work and would lead us to the expectation that the typical "gang" of the adolescent would tend, by unconscious preference, to contain five members, or multiples of this number. In other terminology we might say that the gestalt of the adolescent gang would tend most strongly to "close" at five members.

This brief account presents some of the knowledge gained by recent analytic experience with children carried into puberty and with adolescents carried into adult life. The work was conducted within the framework of theory and technique which is an extension of the developments in psycho-analysis associated with the name of Melanie Klein. It draws very heavily on her delineation of the pre-genital Oedipus conflicts, the role of splitting processes in development, and the phenomenology of projective identification as a dynamic mechanism, and may not be readily comprehended without a general understanding of her work. A most lucid description of this will be found in Hanna Segal's book.

I have discussed how the return of severe splitting processes, characteristic of infancy and early childhood, which attends the adolescent flux, requires externalisation in group life so that the omnipotence and confusional states precipitated by the return of masturbation at puberty may be worked through. The implications for sociological comprehension of the "adolescent world" as a social institution are apparent:

(1) Individual psychotherapeutic work should be directed toward the isolated individual, to promote the socialisation of his conflicts.

(2) The "gang" formation of adolescents needs to be contained in its anti-social aspects but not to be intruded upon by adult guidance.

(3) The emergence of individuals from adolescence into adult life is facilitated by measures which lessen the conflict between the sexual aspirations toward mating and other areas of ambition.

CHAPTER 8

The Emergence from Adolescence

IT is evident that psycho-analysts use the term "adolescent", as they should use all technical terminology, in a metapsychological sense particularly to signify a global state of personality. While we understand it to be statistically related to the years following pubescence, we should not limit ourselves to a chronological vertex but rather to consider that, like any developmental organisation, adolescence is likely to persist until it is abandoned either by progression or by regression. When the regression is to a strongly pathological organisation of earlier development, the differentiation of these two outcomes may be very obvious, but when it is a return to a fairly well organised latency period as the status quo ante, the distinction between progress and regression may be lost to direct observation and only become apparent in the course of psycho-analytical work. This proves to be the case with many people who come to psycho-analysis for professional motives. It is too glib and disrespectful to write off these motives as rationalisations; the professional aspects, the admiration for psycho-analysis as a science, the wish to utilise its findings or to contribute to its development are often quite genuine. This is to be differentiated from the approach of people suffering from the disorders of pseudo-maturity to which I have referred elsewhere (1966), (1967) in which there is a serious impediment to adolescent development as the consequence of a spurious or even fraudulent approach to the adult world. In referring to people who regress to latency rather than progress to adult organisation, and in mentioning the covert quality of this step backwards, I imply no fraudulent motive, but only retreat to mechanisms by which peace was purchased earlier in the face of oedipal suffering, now resorted to again in the face of new suffering in the realm of sexuality.

I have indicated in Chapter 7 that the central turmoil in adolescence is one of confused identity related to the re-emergence of the severe splitting of the self, so characteristic of pre-oedipal and pregenital periods of infancy and early childhood. This mechanism is deployed in puberty to cope with the tidal wave of genital craving in all its polymorphous and perverse infantile forms, as yet little modified by the adult self and introjective identification. From the homosexual gang-formation of puberty, the heterosexual pairing-group of adolescence arises. Through this grouping the couples bob to the surface of adult life. Emphasis must be placed on the function of the coupling in development, for, where sexual intimacy is not stabilised sufficiently for an atmosphere of potential parenthood to enter into the relationship, further development of the personality is severely impeded in both members. Where it does enter, development can be seen to commence to marshall its forces in *both*.

For personality development, unassisted by external therapeutic agencies, tends to proceed beyond adolescence in pairs or not at all, like the embarkation from the Deluge. Since the same tide of sexuality which destroys the structure of the latency period also promotes the object-hunger of puberty and adolescence, a crucial period of years—late 'teens and early twenties—writes "urgent" to this coupling. Time and again we see in the consulting room those in their thirties who have missed the boat and, having lost now the object hunger, must rely on more negative motives such as revulsion against loneliness, deprivation and ostracism. They must drive themselves slavishly rather than being sped forward by the dream of an ideal object. Often the tardy marriage of convenience is already in disarray when they arrive and the analysis must proceed under the most stressful circumstances. Having maintained, at best, a semblance of sexual intimacy through the various devices of pseudo-potency, they are obliged to let go one handhold before having established another, a task to which their courage is often unequal.

A talented young musician came to analysis in his thirties after a successful career had begun to be crippled by claustrophobic symptoms and hypochondriacal states. His success had commenced early in his 'teens when his talent as a performer enabled him to leave school and earn a great deal of money. His greed was rationalised as need to support a beloved mother who had brought him out of Eastern Europe where political changes had swallowed his liberal politician father. Earlier, his father had already been absent for long periods of political imprisonment and the child's relation to his mother had been a highly idealised, romantic, possessive one.

When her beauty had brought her admirers in the new country, the adolescent boy turned from her to a promiscuous life, compulsive and polymorphous, degraded but not essentially perverse. Nonetheless, his compulsive responsiveness to the sexual demands of women drew him into perversity, the anal sadistic components of which led to his gradual breakdown.

But a far more important factor for the breakdown in his late twenties was the rejuvenation of his capacity for love, manifested by a renewed closeness to his mother and a continuing and affectionate relation to a woman in all obvious respects quite opposite to his mother in personality and appearance. With the warming of his intimate life, a disgust with the purely commercial and entertainment quality of his work arose, setting up widening circles of interest and creative desire.

As his mounting symptomatology cut him off from his old career and hampered the development of a new one, analysis was grasped at with desperation—but with courage. The early treatment yielded him quick returns in proportion to his urgent abandonment to co-operation. But as his claustrophobia and hypochondria receded, the priggishness, obsessional and sterile, of his latency period tended to return. It became clear in dream after dream that his wife and his mother stood in relation to one another as part-object to whole-object. His wife could be seen to represent the breast, sometimes genital, sometimes buttock, often containing also a little-girl part of himself in projective identification.

This period in analysis, during which he had renounced his polymorphous and perverse infantile sexuality but not yet developed full adult potency, had a structure perfectly illustrated by a dream which, as a landmark of the analysis, became known subsequently as the "Family Park" dream. In the dream, *couples were rolling about on the ground in various states of drugged and sexual ecstasy, in a barbed-wire enclosure. He was one of them, but unlike the others, noticed the approach of Negroes with machine guns and was able to leap over the barrier before the slaughter commenced. He then found himself on a promenade between the barbed wire and the fence of a family park, to which he could not gain entrance as he had no ticket. But he could see the parents and children within.*

The following 16 months of analysis witnessed very great changes in his life outside analysis, including the birth of his first child and great strides in his new career. But his manliness did not progress in the sexual area, where a relative impotence and poverty of imagination coupled with mounting jealousy of his wife's friendships, with men and women alike, seriously impaired the joy in the emerging family. Dream after dream revealed his projective identification with the child, his possessiveness of the mother and denigration of the father. In fact it became clear that his behaviour as father and husband was greatly controlled by the little boy's demands. In a word, he behaved as house-boy, even tending to withdraw from his wife's bed.

In the transference, his resistance to having a father took the form of argumentativeness, a new secretiveness, obstinacy about readjusting the very low fee to his improved income, and a general attitude of suspicion about analysis. He wondered if it was not really a new "religion", and often experienced the analyst to be demanding unquestioning belief and unreserved dependence.

In the final four months of this sixteen months period the patient's mounting resentment of the analytic procedure was accompanied by dream after dream where he rejected men in authority, regardless of their benevolence. Ultimately he even dreamed, for the first time in his memory, of his father, as he must in fact have been. In the dream, *his father presented himself but the patient rejected the relationship as bogus. The father said he could prove it and gave him a pair of shoes to try. They fitted perfectly and the patient was at first astonished, but then stubbornly insisted that it proved nothing.*

The last ditch stand of the resistance produced three weeks full of drunkenness and brazenness, bitter complaints and threats of interruption. It broke only on the eve of the Christmas holiday, with a dream in which *his mother complained, her hand to her heart, that she could no longer bear his selfishness.*

Only with this collapse of his infantile omnipotence, in the face of the depressive concern about the mother, did a satisfactory differentiation of adult and infantile arise in the sphere of his masculinity. The wonder-boy receded and the man took his place in the analytic co-operation, in his home and in his work. The delicate balance between regression and progression decisively tipped. What his adolescence had so tenaciously gripped, as a continuation of his oedipal triumph of early childhood, later reinforced by the father's death, at last yielded to depressive realisation of the pain inflicted on his object—and in the outside world on the analyst. In reality, his mother took great pleasure in serving as baby sitter, and undoubtedly doted on her son and grandson while the memory of her troubled marriage grew dim in her mind. But a father had returned to the patient's inner world.

This material, in its exaggeration due to traumatic factors (loss of the father in latency) and pathogenic influence (the mother's passivity toward the boy), illustrates in bold relief the fundamentals of adolescent turmoil and its poised position between progression to adult organisation and regression to latency rigidity, or more pathological organisation. The highly possessive, controlling and erotised relationship to his mother before puberty had resulted in severe anxiety, sexual inhibition and idealisation of women in puberty from which the youth had wrenched himself by a near-psychopathic manoeuvre. Opportunism in his profession and unprincipled predatory sexual behaviour formed the cornerstones of an adolescent adjustment which lasted late into his twenties. Its foundation in a narcissistic collusion was made clear early in analysis through dreams of reversible overcoats or books disguised by differing dust-jackets. This "turncoat" trickiness implemented a precarious balance between fidelity to his maternal good object and membership of the delinquent gang. They began to threaten him in dreams, coming to be known as the "razor-blade gang", as soon as he took a stand against the acting-out of the opportunism and promiscuity, and their being acted-in in the transference through dishonesty about the fees and witholding of material.

The foundation of this adolescent organisation lay in the rejection of differentiation between adult and infantile sexuality, coupled with zonal confusions. The need of a father was obviated by these means, so that feeding her precious boy was deemed sufficient gratification for the internal mother—both in her genital and breast. This was clarified by dreams such as: *a young woman lay naked on the breakfast table offering her succulent genital.* He remembered with defiant pride his mother's argument against his latency modesty. "A husband is a stranger but a child is one's own flesh and blood."

Omnipotence in its many facets was the stabilising force in this precarious balance, variously controlling, seducing and gratifying good objects while deceiving, placating and exploiting his persecutors of the gang, both in dreams and in acted-out pattern. In the absence of a stabilised introjective identification, projective identification was occasionally resorted to for purposes of identity but more often entry into the mother's body was undertaken for refuge or in order to control her. His identity was built around the gifted, tricky, erotic and greedy little-boy part of his personality. It all began to crumble when love for his future wife and accompanying revulsion against his promiscuous and unprincipled life began to gain the upper hand, producing anxiety, claustrophobia and hypochondriacal symptoms related to the dying state of the father-imprisoned-in-the-rectum and the deprived-and-debilitated-mother-in-his-heart. The latter produced acute attacks of cardiac anxiety, the basis of which is clear in the dream of his mother, holding her heart, complaining of the patient's selfishness. The former situations produced occasional acute attacks of pain in the rectum, deep in the pelvic cavity.

In summary, then, this material is drawn upon to illustrate the essence of adolescence, how, following the pseudo-heterosexual gang-formation of puberty, an attempt is made to break out of the restrictions of sexuality imposed by the latency organisation and to achieve heterosexual potency without recourse to introjective identification. The adolescent attempts to by-pass the working through of the depressive anxieties which are prerequisite to the establishment of internal objects of full potency. The turning-point is not difficult to discern in analytic material, but even less penetrating techniques of investigation may reveal that the urge toward parenthood, in its many facets, the "family park" sexuality, tips the balance between regression to latency rigidity and progression to adult potency in introjective identification with the combined object.

CHAPTER 9

The Introjective Basis of Polymorphous Tendencies in Adult Sexuality[1]

THIS chapter is an attempt to bring some greater order into the area of sexual theory by helping to differentiate the basis of adult polymorphous sexual tendencies from the imperious incursions, of pathological significance, which contaminate the adult sexual life. They come from areas of polymorphous and perverse infantile sexuality. In order to do this in a way that will have immediate validity for the consulting room, I plan to discuss both the technical and theoretical problems separately and then relate them one to the other.

Technical Problems

It would be a plausible deduction from the psycho-analytic theory of personality development that sexual behaviour does not need to be taught, but derives its form from instinctual drives modified by identification processes. Sexual education, therefore, has no precise place in the psycho-analytical method, which aims to bring about integration and differentiation in psychic structure in order that learning by experience may take place. In all our patients, regardless of age, the clinical material presents us with the task of assisting in the differentiation of levels in psychic life. Our business is the analysis of the infantile transference with the co-operation of the more advanced and most mature mental structures.

In the realm of sexuality this becomes a pressing problem immediately puberty commences and the urgency of genital desire makes itself felt in the transference. The experience of carrying a latency child in analysis into puberty highlights the terrible chaos of levels, zones, and identifications that the pubertal process produces. But in grown patients, whether the genital life has piogressed no further than masturbation, or has settled into a stable heterosexual mating, the problem of differentiating analytically between the adult sexual life and the intrusive infantile substructures must go on even though our attitude toward the content of the adult activities is simply one of putting them aside as not in themselves the concern of

[1] Read to the British Psycho-analytical Society, published in the Scientific Bulletin, No. 10, 1967.

psycho-analytic investigation. In a sense this is a simple function of tact and respect for privacy. Fortunately we have a perfect method for making this differentiation, namely the primary rule, which imposes no task of selection on the patient but rests on the assumption that anything he observes going on in his mind in the consulting room has arisen because it has some relevance to the infantile transferences, however slight or obscure. If this is well understood by the patient, he is in a position to know when he is withholding material. The analyst, on the other hand, cannot *know* this, he can only deduce it from behaviour, gaps in the data, or indications in the patient's dreams.

This clarification by primary rule leaves the analyst merely the task of separating adult and infantile aspects of the material, with the tacit acknowledgment to his patient that what is adult and private is of no analytic concern. However, this process of differentiation seems to be difficult for a particular reason with which this paper is chiefly concerned, namely, that analytic theory has not as yet made clear the parameters of adult sexuality so that its richly polymorphous nature can be surely distinguished from the proliferating polymorphism and perversity of infantile sexuality.

When I say that the adult sexual life is private I do not mean that I have any illusion that it is conflict-free. Psycho-analysis has no aspiration to free people of conflict but rather to equip them for resolving current conflicts. This it does by freeing them from the compulsion to repeat conflicts of the past (transference) and, eventually, by strengthenihg the structure of the personality so that learning from experience can take place (Bion). This is extremely important for an analyst to appreciate in order to avoid being drawn as mentor, mediator or judge into the patient's external relations. In no area is the pressure more severe than in connection with sexual life.

Theoretical Problems

Freud's differentiation of source, aim and object in infantile sexuality seems stark, if not moralistic. He elevates heterosexual genitality to a unique position, as if it were the only aspect of infantile sexuality fit to survive into adult life. Abraham's clarification of the distinction between part- and whole-object relations enriched the conception of genital sexuality, but did nothing to alter the quantitative and normative attitude implied. Instead of clearly defining the state of mind involved in the adult love relationship, it tended to exalt an act of genital coitus, rampant on a field of pregenital foreplay, a sort of coat of arms of the sexual aristocracy.

But it is necessary to remember that this conception arose before the investigation of psychic structure had even begun, and before the psycho-analytic method of investigation of psychic events had been developed into a reliable tool. In many ways the "Three Essays on Sexuality" is more descriptive than metapsychological. Today, some 40 years after the publication of "The Ego and the Id", our knowledge of psychic structure and the nature of internal and external object relations is considerably advanced, certainly far enough for a renewed effort in the area of sexual theory. To begin with, knowledge of splitting processes makes it feasible to draw a structural, rather than descriptive, line between narcissistic organisation and object relations. Further, the distinction between "horizontal" and "vertical" splitting gives a clearer significance on the one hand to the topographic viewpoint of the different levels of psychic life, as well as adding structural firmness to the conception of bisexuality. While we may still agree with Freud that oral and anal phases of development contain only a prelude to sexual differentiation, our understanding of introjective and projective identification gives substance to the terms masculine and feminine as related to parts of the infantile self to a degree that mere reference to Id-constituents could not give. Thus the Oedipus complex may be seen to rise to a crescendo of whole-object and bisexually differentiated drama at four years of age, say, but its significance in babyhood need no longer be doubted. Our language also can now move forward from the descriptive psychiatric basis. A term like "homosexual" can now be given a clear metapsychological significance, if desired, to distinguish it from the manifestations of infantile bisexuality, although there is much to be said in favour of throwing it out as a waste-basket term, as I hope to show, in favour of a more definitive elucidation of the terms *polymorphous* and *perverse* in psycho-analytic theory.

These many improved possibilities of formulation arise from the clearer view we are able to have now, thanks to the light shed by the concept of projective identification as distinct from introjective, on the workings of destructive forces, particularly those connected with envy, which create confusional states, related in particular to the difference between good and bad. By applying this differentiation correctly to the sexual life, internal and external, narcissistic and object-related, part- and whole-object, at all evels of the mental life, we can establish the terms *polymorphous* and *perverse* as having definitive reference to good and bad sexuality respectively. In this sense they refer to the libidinal and destructive drives but also to the splitting process (splitting-and-idealisation) by which good and bad parts of self and objects are established and differentiated in unconscious phantasy.

By means of these three dimensional differentiations, libidinal and destructive impulses, adult and infantile sexuality, good and bad parts of self and objects, the way is made clearer in analytic work for resolving the terrible confusions which erupt in puberty and are seldom satisfactorily clarified outside analysis. Although it is not the purpose of this paper to classify the disturbances of sexual life met with in analytic practice, I offer the following as a restatement of these theoretical views in clinical terms as a guide.

Perversions   (a) Expressions of narcissistic organisation (sado-masochistic)

(b) Defences against depressive anxieties (inverted object choice and zonal confusions)

Polymorphisms

Inhibitions   (a) Due to excesses of persecutory anxiety, almost always coupled with some form of narcissistic masturbatory perversion

(b) Due to excesses of depressive anxiety, usually connected with intense splitting of the bi-sexuality (obsessional)

Immaturities (a) Poor differentiation of adult and infantile polymorphous tendencies

(b) Intensified polymorphous tendencies due to infantile zonal confusions

(c) Inadequate genital responsiveness due to defective introjective identification (identification with defective objects—closely related to obsessional type of inhibition)

It is important to note that any one of the above may give rise to a sexual pattern deserving the descriptive term "homosexual", which illustrates its virtual uselessness in psycho-analytic nosology.

This brings us to the real substance of this paper, a description of the unconscious basis in introjective identification for the polymorphous tendencies in adult sexuality. While I do not plan to substantiate the description here, it is hoped that the conception will immediately make links for readers with their own clinical material. It has been built up over a period of years from my own adult and child cases, neurotic and psychotic, as well as from supervisory work with other analysts and students.

The foundation, in the unconscious, of the sexual life of the mature person is the highly complicated sexual relation of the internal parents, with whom he is capable of a rich introjective identification in both masculine and feminine roles. A well-integrated bisexuality makes possible a doubly intense intimacy with the sexual partner by both introjection as well as a modulated projective identification which finds its place in the partner's mentality without controlling or dominating. It is akin to the normal use of projective identification as a primal mode of communication, as described by Bion (1963), and differs greatly, therefore, from the violent splitting and projective identification of the infantile bisexuality which is so prevalent in puberty and adolescence, epitomised in "the crush".

In order, therefore, to understand the complex structure of affects, impulses, phantasies and anxieties which make up the adult sex life, we must turn our attention to the nature of the coital relation of internal parents, as we are able to construct it from psycho-analytical data. The first principle that must be understood is that the coital relation of internal objects has an overwhelming relation to that dependence of infantile parts of the self on the internal mother which is the foundation of all stable and healthy psychic structure. This dependence we know to be of two sorts: in the first instance, on the mother's capacity to receive the projection of infantile states of mental and physical distress, experienced as persecution by bodily contents, especially the faeces and urine. In psychic reality all persecutions coming from outside the infant's body are experienced as secondary to the expulsion of those contents. The baby depends on the mother's capacity to return to it parts of the self, which have been then divested of all persecutory qualities, by means of the feeding relation to the breast. In connection with these two primal functions of the internal mother, her dependent relation, in turn, to the internal father and his penis and testicles is experienced as essential for her survival, and for the survival of the babies-inside-the-internal-mother whose welfare is felt to be a prerequisite for her generosity and benevolence. Although in its earlier form, at a part-object level, the breast is felt to have both toilet and feeding functions, at whole-object levels the division of top and bottom of the mother's body expresses the need in the infant to feel certain that its excreta can be kept well separated inside the mother from her breast and milk. Her body therefore comes, in unconscious phantasy, to have three delimited spaces, top, front-bottom and back-bottom, corresponding to breast, genital and rectum.

The inside of the mother's body is felt furthermore to acquire penis-like structures from coitus with the father which subsequently, by forming part of her own equipment, perform various functions in these three spaces. These functions are of two types, keeping order and protecting. Thus the flow of milk is felt to be regulated by a nipple-penis. The separation of the three spaces is carried on by policing functions of inside-penises. The expulsion of intruders is a well-known sub-type of these protective functions seen in the claustrophobic anxieties. The sphincter of each space, mouth, introitus and anus, is experienced as an inside-penis of the mother.

In contrast to these inside-penises, without testes, the penis of the father, with testes, is felt to have a reparative role in which the semen is the essential factor. Furthermore, the three spaces are felt to have each a specific relation to the father's penis-and-testicles (genital) by way of one of the three orifices of the mother's body, the introitus, the anus and the mouth. Thus the semen is felt to feed the babies in the genital, to flush out and purify the rectum and to supply raw materials for the production of milk.

During the analytic process, after the relation to the breast has been more firmly established, while the Oedipus complex at its various levels is being worked over and resolved, this relationship between the internal parents can be studied in detail. During the analytical working-through one form of infantile attack and intrusion after another is relinquished under the pressure of the depressive concern for the welfare of the object. But even after all the facets mentioned above have been allowed to find their correct place, the last-ditch stand of envy and jealousy entrenches itself against the blossoming of pleasure in the midst of utility; for at infantile levels pain and pleasure are insistently held to be affects appropriate to work and play respectively.[1]

Clinical Material

A man of intelligence and some distinction in his academic field, married and with three children, sought analysis for hypochondriacal complaints of acute onset. The only boy, youngest of three, having lost his father in puberty, he had assumed a distant, administrative and trustee relation to his mother as he progressed through adolescence. His character from an early time had had the "pseudo-mature" structure,[2] genteel, snobbish, dilettantish, a great seducer of married women at the level of dinner table conversation, but fundamentally impotent. A stony paranoid attitude toward men and a dread of homosexual temptation was eased socially by a placating demeanor, but a deep contempt for masculinity gave force to a persistent masturbatory phantasy of finding two policemen together in a police car, handling or sucking one another's genitals. We recognised only in the third year of analysis, when the policemen-nipple turned up in dreams, that this persistent voyeurist phantasy represented the nipples, together in the brassiere, feeding and delighting one another.

---

[1] See Chapter 17 for further elaboration of this theme.
[2] See my paper on Anal Masturbation (1966).

This understanding relieved a perverse tendency which had dogged him since the latency period, in one form or another.

However, no relief came to the impotence which had become manifest when his wife's loss of desire after the third child released him from the demands he had been only able to meet by the device of pseudo-potency based on secret employment during coitus of the phantasies of his perversion.

From early in the analysis the internal mother's body had always appeared as houses, churches and gardens, to which he had a proprietory, executive or custodial relation. The first two years of analytic work added the field of psycho-analysis to this list and gave rise to the acting out of psycho-therapeutic demeanour in his external relations and a Boswell-to-Johnson relation in the trans-ference to the analyst-daddy, while in dreams his own father's grave, separated by some miles from his mother's house, became a frequent representation. It was clear that he functioned in a state of projective identification with a father's penis, alive but detached as a part-object from the rest of the dead father.

As his projective identification, and the pseudo-maturity attending it, yielded to the analysis of the numerous anal-masturbatory habits which reinforced it, the dependent relationship at a toilet-breast level was strengthened and the many areas of zonal confusion came under fruitful investigation. His mother began regularly to appear in his dreams, generally old and ill, while his wife became a regular representative, in dream and acting out, of the little-girl aspect of his infantile bisexuality. His father began at rare intervals to appear in his dreams, to his great relief and pleasure, and the pain of his father's death, put off so abruptly after an hour's crying at the news in puberty, was little by little accepted, with dreadful pain at moments —and with associated fears of his analyst dying.

But his objects were still held in rigid obsessional control and kept well-separated internally, so that hypochondriacal rumination, as distinct from the hypochondriacal crises which brought him to analysis, became a persistent feature. At this time the voyeurist phantasies and masturbatory practices tended to reappear at times of separation in the transference, and the narcissistic organisation underlying it could be studied.

Once the narcissistic organisation could be abandoned as a defensive position and replaced by dependence on the analytic breast as a reparative object in relation to his internal world, a process was set in train which illustrates the subject of this paper. With the surrender of this area of narcissism and of the attendant omnipotent (manic) reparative projective identification with the split-off father's penis as a part object, the internal father, and the analytic father in the transference, began to take on qualities of genital potency which, for the first time in the patient's life since the age of four, produced an introjective identificatory stimulus to his genital heterosexuality. The relatively vigorous oedipal period in childhood had been traumatically crushed by a prolonged separation from his mother due to illness, placing an excessive strain on a genital development which was not adequately founded, since his oral and anal pregenitality had been unsound, as manifest by feeding difficulties, tantrums, and intolerance to contamination.

The fifth year of analysis was particularly marked by a series of dreams in which the figure of paternal potency appeared in numerous reparative, regulatory and vitalising roles, while his mother became steadily less ill, younger, more beautiful and more warm in his dreams. His adult character could be seen to alter correspondingly, as the snobbery was replaced by humility, the loathing and contempt for work by industry, the custodial relation to his mother by one of warm concern, the doll-house marriage by a struggle to find a manly emotional relation to his wife and the need to be idealised by his children changed to closer paternal contact with their emotionality.

This lengthy preamble has been necessary to set off the significance, germane to this paper, of the dream representations of the manifold functions of the paternal genitals, penis and testicles, as they were gradually allowed to establish themselves in psychic reality.

DREAM—At a dinner party given by an unmarried woman analyst, a bachelor clergyman appears. As the patient goes to fetch a chair for him, he pauses to admire a plant, a "potentilla", but accidentally knocks off some of its blossoms.

DREAM—He feels resentful of a fiftyish Australian man who insists on standing watch behind him while the patient is defecating into a toilet in the middle of a tea room.

DREAM—He is in the cabin of a paddle-wheel boat with his mother, who is looking young and well. He feels that a storm has torn the ship from its moorings, captainless, but when he rushes on deck he finds no storm. The ship is still firmly tied to the quay.

DREAM—A BBC woman tells him that in Senegal everything is in threes—Senegal, Senegal, Senegum (associations—"All Gaul is divided into three parts"; a storybook of childhood about a little steam engine who tried very hard, always puffing, "I think I can, I think I can").

DREAM—The analyst's carpenter is making a grille for the French door of the patient's home, but shows them how a sponge cake has three layers of jam in one part. The patient wonders how he put it there.

DREAM—He wants to show his wife on a map of Ireland the island his mother visited with a girl friend when young, but that part is

*missing and he can only find a peninsula with the village of "Bisto"
on it.*

Such examples from the year's work could be multiplied but the
point is, I believe, sufficiently illustrated. We see clergyman-
daddies with potentilla penises and blossom testicles; fiftyish
Australian-daddies to supervise his "down-under" relation to the
toilet-mummy; captain-daddies who keep boat-mummies firmly tied
to reality; communicating analyst-BBC-mummies who encourage
little boys to grow up to be proper Caesar-daddies with relation to all
three orifices of a woman's body with all three parts, penis and testes;
carpenter daddies who know how to protect mummy's French door-
vagina and still fill her sponge-breast with jam-semen; of analytic
maps which show that mummy's island-breasts don't go on holiday
with one another but with daddy's Bisto-penis; etc., etc.

Clinical Reference

When this aspect of psychic reality, the complexity of the coital
relationship of internal objects, is clearly before us, we are in a
position to understand the polymorphous nature of adult sexuality
and to sort it out from infantile and perverse elements in our patient's
material. Identification with the internal parents gives rise to strong
fellatio impulses, which need to be distinguished from infantile
turning-to-the-penis-as-an-oral-object or confusion of nipple and
penis. The intimate link between father's mind, tongue, language,
penis and semen gives strong erotic significance to language and the
tongue, which must be distinguished from infantile confusion of
tongue and penis as the tool of oral satisfaction. Bodily juxta-
positions such as coitus a tergo, derive from the identification with
the internal father cleaning the mother's rectum, and must be
distinguished from anal-sadistic perverse impulses which produce
the fæcal-penis and assaults on the anus. The importance of the
testicles and the ejaculation of the semen becomes understandable in
terms of identification, so that it can more surely be distinguished
from those infantile preoccupations with the semen which accompany
the denigration of the breast and milk. The place of the testicles in
adult sexuality can be better comprehended, distinguished from the
more phallic preoccupation at infantile levels. Disturbances in
attitude toward menstruation, including sado-masochistic excitement, come clearly to light when juxtaposed to the relative increase
in sexual desire at this time, based on identification with a soiled and
disappointed internal mother. The invigorating effect of adult
coitus can be sharply differentiated from the inevitable deterioration
of the mental state ensuing from the acting out of infantile masturbatory phantasies during sex relations. When circumstances

deprive a healthy person of a love partner, the bisexuality generates a masturbatory pressure which is easily distinguishable, in dream and phantasy, from the infantile autoerotisms.

One final word might be said about the implication of these discoveries about psychic reality to distinguish them from morality. Introjective identification with the combined object induces a bond of mutuality and shared responsibility for the children, of a character that favours monogamy.

Summary

In this chapter I have tried to pull together recent accumulation of knowledge about the relationship of the internal father and mother to one another, as it emerges in the process of integration within the depressive position in the later phases of successful analysis, in order to construct a coherent picture of the introjective basis of the polymorphous aspects of adult sexuality. It is the theme of this chapter that such a scheme makes for surer **and** more tactful work in the analysis of the areas of sexual disturbance in all our patients, even the children. It should also enable us to construct a truly metapsychological nosology of sexual pathology to replace the descriptive one inherited from neuropsychiatry.

CHAPTER 10

The Genesis of the Super-ego-Ideal

RATHER than pause to explain the elision of super-ego and ego-ideal in the title, let us press on to the substance, hoping that by the end its significance will have become clear.

Freud took an evolutionary view of psychic structure and nothing in our scientific findings since his time militates against his thesis. The ego has evolved from the id by specialisation of function and the super-ego-ideal has evolved from the ego in like manner. Nothing speaks against this view, but what is the evidence *for* it? The answer is surely, "The totality of the psycho-analytical process!". It is the phenomenon par excellence of our study, but as our method concerns itself particularly with psychopathology through study of the disturbances in the evolution of the transference, we are prone to overlook the wealth of evidence it lays before us regarding psychic health and growth. It is true that in our methodological pre-occupation with the disturbances of the transference we operate on the assumption that by removing the obstacles to growth and by blocking divergent pathways of development we make it possible for the vital processes to push on unaided. But while cogent in theory, this often does not happen in fact. Something akin to what Freud called "psychic inertia" so opposes growth that an input of vitality in the form of analytic determination is required during the working through periods.

Clinical Material

The first three years of a male patient's analysis had been very fruitful in resolving the problems of projective identification which had, since early childhood, imposed a pseudo-mature character upon him, manifest in smugness, pomposity, hypochondria and im-poverished interests and imagination. Obsessive difficulties and a variety of minor phobias had yielded to the analysis of zonal confusions and of his strong passive anal trends. But the approach to the depressive position was bogged down in a prolonged period of inertia, well-characterised by a dream in which *he was lying in bed in his hotel room at a resort, knowing well that the checking-out time was past, but when the manageress entered and asked him to leave, he did nothing. The sun was either rising or setting.*

At this time his paternal object still appeared very denigrated, the "shit jacket daddy" of innumerable dreams in which shabby clothing and low vitality were characteristic, coupled however with benign and helpful qualities. His father's actual lack of financial success and his exemption from military service in both wars still anchored a relentless denigration of a man in whom the patient could otherwise find no fault and toward whom he felt a distinctly feminine love.

The struggle with his inertia, his holiday on my couch, went on for about two years, but progress was manifest in gradual changes of the paternal figure in dreams, in the transference, in his attitude to his actual father and in his character outside the analytic situation. Still, the inertia remained in his behaviour in the analysis. He was content to bring whatever material welled up in free association, letting the analyst do all the interpretative work—and all the worrying—while he mightily enjoyed the apparently interminable process.

But feelings of inferiority began slowly to emerge and with them a growing interest in, and concern about, the world. Phobias gone, he became more aware of a diffuse cowardice in his relationships, a general evasiveness toward conflict, a placation of aggression in others and difficulty in formulating views and convictions of his own.

Two dreams, 12 months apart, illustrate the gradual change which ensued. In the first dream the patient (who was a young doctor at this time in fact considering applying for analytic training) *found himself wading into the sea following a tall man dressed in a sou'wester. In the distance there seemed to be a milk bottle, either floating or partly submerged. As the water became deeper, the patient felt panic that at any moment he might become unable to touch bottom and would be swept away by the current.*

One year later he dreamed that *Dr Ball, who seemed to be the new professor of another department, appeared unexpectedly in an informal visit to the patient's ward. He was immensely pleased but a bit nervous, as Dr Ball was a man he greatly admired for his integrity, for his devotion to his patients and his clinical experience—but in a field different from the patient's. The two nurses were a bit annoyed but greeted Dr Ball with respect—they were middle-aged, not sexually attractive but efficient and friendly.*

We have, then, two images: (1) patient, man in sou'wester, milk bottle; (2) patient, Dr Ball, two nurses. Panic in one, pleasure mixed with nervousness in the other.

At the time of the first dream, after six years of analysis, his illness was largely a thing of the past. He had a firm foot in the depressive position, his acknowledgement of psychic reality was good, and some considerable distance had been covered in the resolution of his direct and inverted oedipus complex. What remained, in addition to the process of bringing the analysis to a close, was the residual immaturity manifest by a slight boyishness, by dependence on the opinions and ideas of others and consequent slowness to take up responsibilities, though in fact he carried well the heavy ones thrust upon him. The boredom and lack of direction which had led him to analysis had been replaced by a rich participation in professional and family life, a wide intellectual interest and a good capacity for pleasure at work and play. He was respected, liked, even loved—a good friend and an ethical opponent. But something was lacking which undermined his stability and nipped creative imagination in the bud.

It could be seen, of course, that much room for development and integration at infantile levels still remained. His femininity was not fully integrated but still easily split off and projected. His destructive part, while seldom projected outward, was held inwardly in an unintegrated state, outside the sphere of the breast. But these matters, one could reasonably hope, would improve with time and self-analysis if the quality of his adult organisation was right for fully assuming the burdens that had been carried by the analyst.

In fact something was wrong there which the first dream makes very clear. In the dream he is in a *following-in-daddy's-footsteps* relation to his good paternal object and following it to a *goal*—the milk bottle. We knew much about this figure in the sou'wester already and its origins in a film he had seen as a boy, "Captains Courageous". We also knew that "touching bottom" meant anal masturbation and seeking refuge in projective identification. We knew also that the milk bottle represented the acceptance of weaning *as a goal*. However it took several sessions of associations and transference material to reveal that his fear of being "swept away" meant swept by a current of passionate interests of his *own*, in a word, by *aims*.

To recapitulate: so long as he was following-in-daddy's-footsteps and concerned with reaching goals, there remained not only a timidity in regard to pursuit of his own interests and desires, but an inability to commit himself to the abandonment of projective identification with internal objects, at times of stress. His goal in life was to become a "real man like daddy". The phallic quality of the masculinity implied in the figure in the sou'wester was clear from many items of association, in which courage in the face of danger was its overriding quality.

If we turn now to the dream of one year later, a rather different spectacle is laid before us. The fact that a Dr Ball did actually exist on the periphery of the patient's professional life and was admired, had recently become professor, etc., should not distract us from recognising the testicular reference. The patient's relationship to this genital father was now a more adult one, *under his aegis* but not *following in his footsteps*. Note the evidence of the patient's femininity—the two middle-aged nurses—being more integrated. Nothing in the dream suggests goals, but only aims, of following his interests and doing his work under the inspiration of the principles of his internal objects—now a combined object—Dr Ball and his professorial chair.

Freud writes, in 1924 in "The Economic Problem of Masochism": "The course of childhood development leads to an ever-increasing detachment from parents, and their personal significance for the super-ego recedes into the background. To the images they leave behind there are then linked the influences of teachers and authorities, self-chosen models and publicly recognised heroes, whose figures need no longer be introjected by an ego which has become more resistant. The last figure in the series that began with the parents is the dark power of destiny which only the fewest of us are able to look upon as impersonal." (*i.e.*—death).

This point, that new qualities become linked to the imagos of the parents, but that the figures of the newer influences need not be introjected, is of immense importance in understanding the modifications of the super-ego and why they are not incompatible with love for the original objects. It is by this means that one's internal objects can not only improve in quality but in scope, so that the aegis they raise in a person's inner world need never be incompatible with interests and desires of the ego, as may easily happen in relation to external parents or mentors.

The point of this material is to illustrate an aspect of the metamorphosis of the super-ego-ideal. Elsewhere* I have described the assimilation to the superego of what I called "equipment" for dealing with the infantile structures, the means of preserving their correct differentiation and of controlling their tendency to regressions to narcissistic organisation. The present material illustrates the transition from "shit-jacket" impotent internal "daddy" to the phallic-courageous "sou'wester daddy", and further to the testicular creative "Dr Ball daddy" as a combined object with his professorship. The factors operative in this metamorphosis are several. The defence against oedipal inferiority through anal-smearing denigration (the "shit-jacket daddy") has gone. The defence against weaning, in favour of a new baby, by means of splitting the testicular-creative function from the phallic-courageous one has desisted. But an introjective factor, manifest in a new interest in history and particularly in the history of psycho-analysis, has implemented a shift

* *The Psycho-analytical Process*, Heinemann, 1967

of values. Where comedians, politicians and military figures had earlier excited his imagination, now artists and scientists, epitomised in the character and accomplishment of Freud, stirred him. He could now consider that, behind the relative obscurity imposed by the technique of analysis, even his own analyst might be a person worthy of his respect. He could not, he realised, even rule out completely the possibility of his being "great".

Freud's fruitful adherence to the great method of investigation he invented brought his inquiries into the nature of mental pain to a culmination in "The Problem of Anxiety". His description of the economic principles of the functioning of the Id, the repetition compulsion, and of the Ego in relation to the Id and the external world, the Pleasure-Pain-Reality Principle, fell short of the problem of value and referred only to the problem of adaptation. It remained for Melanie Klein, in her greatest formulation, the Paranoid-Schizoid and Depressive Positions, to discover the economic principles regulating the relation of Ego to the Super-ego-(ideal) as the foundation of value. This material, as I have said, illustrates the metamorphosis of the super-ego-ideal, through the abandoning of defences, splitting processes, in particular. The acceptance of integration and the assimilation into the super-ego-ideal by introjection also makes clear the paradox, so contrary to common sense, that the most evolved aspect of an individual's mind lies beyond the experience of self and is apprehended as object. The problem with which every theological and philosophical system has attempted to grapple has finally found its proper venue, psychic reality. A new proof of the existence of God has evolved most unexpectedly through an essentially iconoclastic method which has at the same time fused this concept of God with that of individual mind, thus putting an end for all time to the possibility of religion as a social institution beyond the participation of the individual. God is dead in the outside world and brought to life within, but only, as we know, through mourning. It would be a good historical joke if it were to turn out that a Jew had carried the reformation to its logical endpoint.

The paradox remains, that the best aspect of the mind is beyond self and the self must evolve in its relation to its internal objects through dependence, ripening to obedience, and ending as the acceptance of *inspired independence. Under their aegis!* If this theory is correct, the conclusion is inescapable that a man is a fool to defend himself against the mental pains by which disharmony between self and super-ego-ideal is manifest. The spectrum of pains, the pains of the depressive position, herald discord and call for parley, the self-analytic process. The pains are the price we pay for having good objects and, considering their preciousness, they are comically inexpensive. But this should not surprise us since the generosity of the breast is the soul of the combined object.

While the paradox of me and not-me is intriguing, the beauty of the system is rather overpowering in its biology. Where natural selection operates externally, individual selection dominates the growth and change of the super-ego-ideal. As Freud stressed, the *figure* of the internal objects derives largely from the primitive introjection of the parents (modified of course by the contribution of projection and projective identification) during the period of maximal dependence on these external persons. But thereafter introjection of qualities proceeds under the sway of admiration. While cultural influence must be considerable of course, the factor of interest guiding the search for admirable objects must be strongly swayed by aspects of constitution and temperament, which we as yet can hardly explore and can only vaguely name as talents, gifts, tendencies, impulses. We probably think of them, structurally speaking, as attributes of the id, as hereditary, genetically determined, akin to the preconceptions which only await to mate with a realisation to produce a conception, in the notation of Bion. That is, we think of these mental potentialities as residing in the id, awaiting the experiences which will give rise to an ego aspect to which we can then give a specific name—athletic, musical, intellectual, mechanical, etc. It must be this highly individual pattern of potentialities which direct interests and influence admiration in the search for objects for introjection. In this form we refer to them as tastes.

The evolution of tastes was touched upon in the clinical material: where admiration had sought for men of wealth, comedians, politicians and military leaders, it now sought artists and scientists to introject. It was quite clear, in the clinical process, which of these changes came first, that of the super-ego-ideal or the altered tendencies to admiration. The sequence was the following: as narcissistic inertia gave way to depressive concern for the mother, her needs became paramount over the oedipal pain. Her needs then demanded integration of the split-off testicular-creative functions of the father (Dr Ball). Creativity being once established in the internal father, objects recognised as creative in various ways attracted the patient's admiration in the outside world, first of course dead and legendary figures, later live and aged ones and gradually living peers, even perhaps his analyst. These individual and specific qualities could then be seen in dreams to have accrued to his internal father as a whole object and as specific instances of the general quality of creativity already established in the genital part-object relationship to the internal mother, namely, in making her pregnant with the baby who would take the patient's place at weaning. Then at last his interests began to widen, unfettered by envy, carried by an enriched imagination, freed of the one-track-mindedness of projective identification, the narrowness of obsessional rumination or the tentativeness of timidity.

The final realisation must not, however, be obscured by this description of structural progress in analysis. What is "finally" and "at last" achieved in the formal analysis is only the beginning of a development with endless possibilities. Not only is the super-ego-ideal capable of endless assimilation of excellent qualities which it can then help the ego to acquire; it can also be improved structurally, and thus in strength and richness, for the re-integration of the primal splitting-and-idealisation is never complete.

SECTION B

CLINICAL SEXUAL PSYCHOPATHOLOGY

CHAPTER 11

Adult Polymorphous Sexuality

MUCH of the task before us in this Chapter has already been done or adumbrated in Chapter 9, but a certain amount of tracing of implications is still required. It is of particular interest that the psycho-analyst seldom hears much about his patient's adult sexual relationships, since the transference situation draws to it the associations related almost exclusively to the infantile and perverse aspects of sexual behaviour and phantasy currently contaminating the patient's sexual life. For this reason, adherence to the primary rule ensures a tactful preservation of the privacy of the adult love life of the patient, and therefore the privacy of his partner.

Recognition of this fact relieves the analyst of part of the pressure of certain countertransference anxieties, of intrusiveness and meddling, while also placing him in a position to recognise that dutiful reporting of sexual activities by a patient is almost certainly a breach of the primary rule involving an acting-in, and possibly -out, of the transference, in which the sexual partner is being made to represent an excluded part of the infantile self. The analyst need never worry about the content of information being withheld by the patient regarding his sexual behaviour, since the moment such withholding takes place the content itself is no longer to the point: the behaviour of withholding itself needs to be the focus of investigation.

Consequently, a conception of adult sexual states of mind hardly enters into the work of the psycho-analyst for his patients, but it does enter into every patient's (including analysts as former patients) self-analytic work. An adequate analysis should be expected to inculcate the desire, as well as establishing the capacity, for self-scrutiny as a way of life, sleeping and waking, so that the habit of self-observation and evaluation in no way interferes with the capacity for spontaneous response, in emotion as well as action. Its obsessional imitation, so often seen early in analysis, is part of the defensive structure resisting the dependence on parental objects, and is, on the contrary, characterised by a loss of spontaneity of action and of sincerity of emotionality. The resemblance to the pseudo-mature latency child is quite unmistakeable, whether the presenting emotionality is pseudo-grave or pseudo-gay.

83

The primary clue to contamination of a sexual state of mind by infantile or perverse tendencies, is, of course, the intrusion of phantasy into the immediacy of the relationship, especially if the identity of self or partner has clearly been tampered with. Alterations in the setting of the sexual activity is also suspect when it is other than reminiscent, and nostalgic. From the point of view of our investigation, the area of "foreplay" in the descriptive terminology of the "Three Essays" takes on a far more complicated significance. Its natural tendency is ritual in the sense of a celebration of past modes of relationship, since transcended. This area of adult sexuality tends therefore to recapitulate the courtship, in content as well as phantasy, and is thereby the one most likely to be touched by all the infantile and perverse modes of sexual relationships that the union has needed to work through in the process of deepening intimacy and maturation of content.

But the definitive act of coition is serious, not in the sense of minor key, but away from the treble of courtship ritual. It is work, not play, and has a sense of urgent and immediate relation to the stresses of the day, week, era, as the introjective identification, with its cosmic scope, takes hold of the mind-body.

The three-fold structure of the relationship has already been defined in Chapter 9. In its deepest, most basic, primal meaning the woman is in distress and in need and in danger; the man is her servant, her benefactor, her rescuer. She is in distress at the plight of her internal babies, in need of supplies to make the milk for her external babies and in danger from the persecutors her children have projected into her. She needs good penises, and good semen, and must be relieved of all the bad excreta. She will be content, satisfied, safe, while he will be admired, exhausted, exhilarated—triumphant.

Happily this drama lends itself to endless variation, as the endless creativity of artists and scientists proclaim, for it is the foundation of the capacity for work. By this I am not referring to Freud's conception of sublimation, which was really an adjunct to the libido theory.* Furthermore, his line of reasoning, brought to its culmination in "Civilisation and its Discontents", all too strongly suggests that aggression, hedged round by anxiety, compromises in the form of "work". On the contrary, work, or more exactly the impulse to work, is derivative of adult sexuality, the core of which is the preservation-of-the-children. "Preservation of the species" misses the point, which is far more intimate, derived from the introjective identification with the mother and her riches of love (milk) for children. Alongside her generosity the internal father

* See Chapter 18 for further development of this theme.

tends to appear a figure of narrow imagination, directed almost exclusively toward the mother in his concern, more egocentric in his pleasures—of feeling admired and triumphant. The earth-mother, the sun-god-father.

But to return to the point about "preservation of the children". It opens a very important area of investigation. Why "preservation" and not "creation", if we are speaking of identification with earth-mother and sun-god father? How does it come about that this adult sexuality is characterised by humility, modesty, privacy and not by a sense of power and a desire for display? In fact it is the infantile sexuality which craves display and the perversions which generate a sense of power. Why are the real artists too busy working to prattle about creativity? Or, more to the point, why does the artist become inhibited in his work when he is concerned with the exhibition of its products?

The answer is that "creativity" is a function of the internal parents, or the gods, in earlier terminology. Only "discovery" is vouchsafed to the mortals. This is in the very nature of introjective identification, that it is led by admiration of the super-ego-ideal to seek, *in vain*, to be worthy of its inspiration. So different is the delusional quality and consequent pomposity of projective identification! In consequence of this aspirational quality, never to be fulfilled, a constant state of humility is engendered; not necessarily accompanied by feelings of inferiority to any *living* person, but often to the great of the past. Parents, like artists, feel that they have "found", not "created", their children. "It" creates children, just as "it" writes, paints, composes —analyses. "It", the super-ego-ideal, stands outside the experience of "self" as the primal combined object, originally the breast-and-nipple.

CHAPTER 12

Infantile Polymorphous Sexuality

WE are approaching the whole area of sexuality from the point of view of structural theory, claiming that as a tool of investigation it facilitates differentiations which are more germane to the psycho-analytic method of research. We have taken Freud's idea of the primal scene (in phantasy) augmented by the insights of Melanie Klein into the importance of the phantasies, or, in psychic reality, the *facts*, about the inside of the mother's body, as the basic sexual situation, or set. We are classifying states of mind related to sexual activities according to the participation of the self in this primal situation.

The first problem we must broach here, which did not arise in the chapter on adult sexuality, is the problem of identity, or rather the sense of identity. It is clear that the adult sense of identity derives from the introjective identification with parental figures and is fundamentally bisexual, although an individual's integration may not have proceeded so far as to enable bisexuality to be experienced and acknowledged.

In latency also, as described in Chapter 7, an adult part of the personality exists to hold the sense of identity at most times, but the objects of its identifications are so separated, desexualised and diminished in creative vitality on the one hand, and the adult states so alternating with pseudo-mature states induced by projective identifi-cation, that adult sexual states of mind hardly arise. The pot-pourri of adolescent states of mind is hardly worth describing in this respect until our discussion of infantile and perverse states has been accom-plished. Yet it is in the adolescent that the problem of identity is most in evidence. One of the difficulties that lies in the way of the application of our theory is that the adult sexual states of mind, probably in most people, dominate for only the relatively brief period of life when they actually are procreating and rearing their young children, that is, before either settling back into the latency pattern or dissolving into a renewed adolescent state.

However, the phenomenon of identity, the sense of identity, is a moment-to-moment one. As we are describing states of mind in almost purely cross-sectional fashion in relation to time, we are consequently dealing with the situation as experienced by that part of the self which has, for the moment, captured the sense of identity, the immediate "I" and/or "me" of active and passive participation.

From the longitudinal perspective, which concerns the psychiatrist, summation of these states of mind would determine the designation of health, immaturity or illness. The history-taking method of the psychiatrist can be replaced by the observations of the psycho-analytic psychiatrist in the area of rigidity of functions. Therefore when we speak here of infantile polymorphous sexuality, it must not be taken as synonymous with "immaturity" as a psychiatric category. In fact, immature people will be found to experience all sorts of sexual states, in a highly fluid responsiveness to the immediate environment, while all the psychiatric illnesses are characterised by rigidity and constriction, and almost certainly, therefore, by an element of compulsion, although not necessarily of addiction.

To return to our basic set, the primal scene, and its participants: following Freud we can delineate five (we will have to add a sixth when we come to the perversions) members of the family—the two parents, the boy, the girl, the baby-inside-the-mother. Infantile polymorphous states of mind are dominated by the oedipus complex with its jealousy and competitiveness, in search of a solution which does not involve relinquishment of objects and postponement of gratification. Thus, under the pressure of the excitement engendered by sensory evidence of the parents copulating, unable to "face the wall, my darling"*, and sleep, the boy-and-girl-parts either seek to establish their own little marriage or to intrude, disguised as inside-babies, into the parental coitus. The important point which differentiates these infantile states from perverse ones is the motiva-tion, which is basically a good one, to find a resolution for the situation of unfulfilled desire, to some extent, but of the oedipal jealousy and hatred in particular, which are threatening momentarily to swamp the loving and generous attitude toward the good parents. One of the important factors preventing the boy and girl from "facing the wall" is the conviction that the inside-baby is not required to do so, is "privileged" to participate in the parental coitus both in masculine—riding in, or on, daddy's penis, driving the car, riding the horse, shooting the gun, etc.—and in feminine ways—being driven in the car, riding the horse, being protected from the bad fæcal monster, receiving the package from the postman, the milk from the milkman, etc.

---

* This phrase from a well-known children's poem "Four and Twenty Ponies" was used by a child patient of mine to express this situation. In the poem the little girl is promised a dolly if she will "face the wall, my darling, while the gentlemen go by" with "brandy for the parson and 'baccy for the clerk", *i.e.* smugglers.

The other element, in addition to the fact of being driven by excitement and anxiety rather than by need and desire, which characterises the infantile states of mind is the element of zonal confusion. Where adult sexuality is polymorphous in respect of the orifices of the woman in introjective identification with the internal mother's need for penises, semen and evacuation of persecutors, the infantile polymorphous sexuality tends to arise through experimentation for lack of instinctual drive or definitive identification. In lieu of the latter, the infantile sexuality is shaped either by mimicry, born of jealousy, or by projective identification, in which of course the qualities of the mind of the intruder, rather than of the object entered, dominate the phantasy.

In either case, whether inside or outside the mother's body in phantasy, the zonal confusion and experimental ingenuity causes the proliferation of sexual acts through all the permutations and combinations that the various erogenous zones can afford. Nurturing or "making" a new baby, filling the little girl's flat breasts, or saving her from the robbers, murderers, bad animals, etc. in the bad faeces, not yet having concluded that the "good" faeces could not mature into babies—all these purposes are undertaken. But this is play and not work, for the aims are utterly egocentric in relation to the distress of the oedipus complex. Sexual gratification is not a primary aim but arises secondarily, in compensation, when the creative aims fail and are eventually abandoned in favour of pleasure. It is at this point that the theories in the child's mind arise that children are more beautiful than adults, that hairlessness of the genitals is an advantage, that bottoms and not breasts are the source of feminine allure, that the little penis is gem-like and the boy's frenetic vitality is the essence of masculine potency. These denials and assertions, as we have seen, play a very great role in shaping the sexual behaviour of pubertal and adolescent children, en route to being adolescent grown-ups.

When this sensuality replaces the creative aims, infantile greed is of course co-opted strongly and the whole flavour of the infantile polymorphous proliferation becomes more oral, and in that sense regressed. This greed for pleasure, in fact an attitude of having fairly cornered the market on pleasure *vis-à-vis* both grown-ups and children alike, characterises the adolescent sexual flux and accounts for much of the need they feel to flaunt their sexual behaviour. The antithetical juxtaposition of work and pleasure as ideas in the adolescent mentality also derives from this regressive tendency of the infantile polymorphous trends still so active at that age.

Due to the egocentric nature of infantile polymorphous sexuality, two behavioural trends are associated with it: first of all the masturbatory trend, and secondly the tendency to wanton, as distinct from compulsive, promiscuity. The tendency to genital masturbatory expression is particularly prominent where the bisexuality has not been severely split. In general this means that it is more frequent, as compared with sexual play with siblings or other children, where development is healthier and the oedipal attachments strongest. The bisexuality plus the zonal confusions, plus the tendency to employ projective identification phantasies, drives the masturbation in peregrinating fashion from zone to zone, tending to settle into a bimanual front and back, or top and bottom type of play—penis and anus, clitoris and vagina, mouth and anus, etc. As it is experimental in aim, and as experience teaches the child that masturbatory orgasm is followed by depressive and persecutory anxieties, climax is meticulously avoided, and with this avoidance guilt is obviated to a degree which even allows for a certain openness of masturbatory play in young children.

The wanton promiscuity is also a relatively guilt-free activity, in so far as its function is in the service of seeking a resolution of the oedipus complex. Neither guilt for infidelity to original objects nor guilt for seducing others into infidelity to their objects arise to any inhibiting pitch. The spirit of search both for a suitable partner and for the answer to the puzzle of adult (pro)-creativity is taken to legitimise the adventure, providing an adequate plea in mitigation against all impending super-ego indictments. In fact much of the charm of small children and much of the indulgence won by the adolescent community is to be accounted for in this manner.

CHAPTER 13

Infantile Perverse Sexuality

HAVING traversed the "good" and the "naughty" in regard to infantile sexuality, we now come to the area that psycho-analysis knows most about, again because the transference tends naturally to be preoccupied with its endless writhings. As explained, adult sexuality tends automatically to be excluded from the analytic material since it is simply not involved in the transference, while with adult patients the "good" and "naughty" infantile aspects induce so little guilt or other disturbance as to be only touched-on in passing. It is from the small children that our information about infantile polymorphism comes, mainly early in analysis when all the attempts at seduction of the analyst are run through before the transference rhythm really settles down and work commences.

But as perverse sexuality is involved in every aspect of psychopathology, our analytic nets are for ever dredging up references to it. Again we must remember that we are investigating and classifying states of mind, not behaviour, and our point of reference is the "primal scene", as described by Freud and augmented by Melanie Klein. We must now make an additional augmentation. A sixth figure enters upon the scene: the "outsider", the stranger to the family, the enemy of parental creativity, of familial harmony—of love; the evil one, the cynic, the spoiler, the carrier of the mark of Cain.

For personality development to be able to proceed, the primal splitting-and-idealisation described by Melanie Klein must take place, in self and object alike. Upon its accomplishment the primal categories of good and bad depend. Survival of the infant is inconceivable without it, except by the most extreme parasitism equivalent to an amentia. But there are clearly great variations in the quality of the primal splitting-and-idealisation in respect of attributes that might be termed rigidity vs. fluidity, or envisaged as the width of the split, the completeness of it, the sharpness of the cleavage, etc. At any rate what turns up in the analytic material is the existence of a part of the self, merged to a variable extent with a bad part of the object, which is malevolent in its intent toward the primal developmental organisation of idealised parts of the self and idealised objects; that is, toward the "idealised family".

But the attributes of this part of the self are very variable from person to person. Furthermore, Melanie Klein demonstrated in "Envy and Gratitude" that analysis, and by implication good developmental experience in general, is able to produce significant amelioration of the virulence of this part. One of the serious difficulties in the analysis of the very ill patient is, in the first place, that the fusion of this part of the self with bad objects creates the figures of the sadistic super-ego which is clinically difficult to distinguish from the harsh super-ego aspects of part-objects or of damaged objects. Its cult-forming propensity plays a very big part in the crystallisation of perversions and addictions, as we shall see.

But leaving this fusion aside, the bad part of the self varies in attributes from person to person in ways which may be constitutional but often appear to be the consequence of the developmental milieu. The most important of these variable attributes is intelligence, and especially the verbal aspects of symbol manipulation. The impression is often unmistakable that intelligence as a personality attribute can be partitioned and distributed, often very unequally, amongst the parts of the self—unequally in regard to quantity, but also in respect of the various qualities or types of intelligence. This is most strikingly seen, for instance, in the idiot savant tendency to highly specialised virtuosity manifest by some children who have had early autistic disturbance.

On the other hand the bad part may be very muscular, or very sensual, or may have seized upon physical beauty as its main weapon of aggression. But one thing appears certain, those attributes of mentality will tend to be seized and developed for destructive purposes to which the parents in external reality are either most vulnerable or to which they are most blind—which often amounts to the same thing. Where a parent is seriously disturbed and a significant degree of collusion can be established by the bad part of the personality, the situation of fusion to form the sadistic super-ego is most likely. Its clinical manifestation is the *folie à deux* of parent and child, so refractory to analytical therapy.

In general the bad part is able to dominate the entire personality only under certain circumstances. The first of these is that of the sadistic super-ego already mentioned. This seems very largely influenced by developmental milieu. The second seems more constitutional in its origins, though of course this is a category which is bound to be eroded by future research. In this second case the sheer strength of the destructive part seems to overwhelm the personality, as one often feels with paranoid personalities or some psychopaths. But this is such a relative quality. It depends for its hegemony on the relative weakness of the constructive drives and capacity for love, which we know to be very easily attenuated by fortuitous events, such as early illness, separation, deformity.

The third circumstance is of a very different order and very frequently met in the population seeking analysis, namely dominance of the destructive part due to loss of capacity for love as a result of splitting and projective identification. Most frequently a good part has been projected into a younger sibling: in the most severe and rigid cases out of depressive anxiety about a new baby's viability. But most often the projection has taken place as a defence against depressive pain, delegating the capacity for love to an admired sibling. This probably approximates to the "altruistic surrender" described by Anna Freud in "The Ego and the Mechanism of Defence". The motives are not really altruistic although, descriptively, the behaviour emanating from such a sibling relationship often appears in this light.

To a certain extent this mechanism plays a part in the establishment of the latency period and contributes to the fundamental weakness of that type of organisation, particularly its vulnerability to seduction and to the appeal of secrecy. While this is more apparent in boys than in girls, probably the loss of openness and sincerity is equal in the two sexes but differently judged by the grown-ups, to whom the "frogs and snails and puppy dog's tails" quality of boys is more noticeably sadistic than the "sugar and spice" coquetry of little ladies.

"Perversion" (that is: "characterised by perversity of purpose") is a very apt term for the sexual states of mind engendered by the leadership, momentary or fixed, of this destructive part of the personality. Being overwhelmingly influenced by feelings and attitudes of envy toward goodness, generosity, creativity, harmony and beauty of good objects; towards their relationships and the "idealised family" they produce; the destructiveness takes two forms. In the first instance it seeks to destroy these qualities. But that is really too easy to afford much sadistic pleasure. The great satisfaction is in envious competition, which does not emulate but deviates. Negativism, as a quality of impulse (to be distinguished from "negation" as a quality of perception) is not satisfied to refuse; it must do the opposite. "Evil, be thou my good!" is its motto, and under this aegis it wills to create a world which is the negative of everything in nature, in the realm of good objects. The impulses are therefore fundamentally anti-nature and the world it seeks to build is the world of the life-less, for whom the great anxieties of the living, time-bound, cannot exist.

The emotive quality of sadistic perverse sexual states of mind is therefore basically manic. It is not the sensuality that is lusted after but the triumphant abolition of depressive and even persecutory anxiety—depressive above all. By sadistic perversity we must understand those states of mind in which the sense of identity has been invested in (or captured by) the destructive part of the self. We will come later to discuss the masochism of good infantile parts of the personality in neurotic perversity, and the oscillation of the two as compared with fixed states of sado-masochism in the psychotic perversions and addictions.

So much of the structural outcome of the developmental process depends, as Freud correctly predicted, on the economics, and particularly the economics or quantitative aspects of the splitting process. While our researches are still too crude for very definitive statements in this area, certain rough ones can be made with some confidence if we stay very close to the geography of unconscious phantasy. The "width" of splitting-and-idealisation varies between two extremes; at one end of the spectrum the bad part has lodged itself in the mother's nipple and at the other extreme it has been projected into outer space. Both of these are developmentally infeasible, and if intractably held lead to the most severe psychotic disturbances, of paranoid type in the latter instance, and of addiction in the former. Midway between these extremes and least infeasible for development is the position of the "bad" sibling, the black sheep, prodigal son or bad child of the family, whose influence is resisted by the good children while his discipline and education is left to the patience, tolerance and generosity of the parents. This is the situation of optimal integration of the destructive part and has been described by Melanie Klein in "Envy and Gratitude".

This state of integration is probably extremely rare in unanalysed development, its approximation being in the form of a fixed projection of this bad part into an actual sibling, almost always older, who, of course, seldom really deserves the mixture of dread, admiration, hatred and fealty which the position confers upon him. Where the shoe fits, more serious trouble accrues to the development, in inverse relation to the distance of this figure in reality from relatedness to the external parents and in proportion to the chronological age gap between the child and this external figure. For these economic reasons, one of the most noxious figures to turn up in the *dramatis personae* of patients' dreams is the "bad uncle" or "bad aunt", trailing off in virulence, as the age gap narrows and the relatedness widens, to servants, teachers, friends.

But these intimate noxious relationships of childhood are replaceable in adolescence by figures of repute where the quality of relatedness to parents is substituted by the quality of fame in the realm of art, literature, politics, religion, entertainment. These external figures achieve their harmful significance by the process of re-projection of earlier relationships which had been abandoned and internalised as part of the establishment of latency. This not only pertains to public figures who are themselves in fact abandoned to cynicism and destructiveness, to fraud and corruption, but also to those creative figures in whom a sad gap exists between the value of their public works and the chaos of their private relationships. The romantic bent of adolescence keenly asserts a causal relationship between the two realms, being unable to see that they are related to a common source, one a product of successful struggle with conflict and the other a failure or even abandonment of struggle.

So much of economic importance in the progress of development depends on the attitude toward mental pain. And indeed one might say that the vulnerability of the "good" parts of the infantile structure rests upon it as one of the three great economic factors. The other two are the degree of integration of the good parts and the level of trust in good objects. The hierarchic relation of the three to each other, however, seems to be in an inverse order, chronologically; trust influences the degrees of integration which in turn influences the attitude toward pain.

Trust in good objects, basically the mother's breast, is an area that has been too extensively investigated and described by Melanie Klein to bear any repetition here. She has demonstrated over and over again the way in which the operation of projection and introjection by the infant, modified by the actual qualities of the external mother in her care of the baby, builds up an idealised breast internally as the centre of dependence and the core of hopefulness. Bion and Winnicott, in their individual ways, have described the qualities of mind and behaviour, respectively, which make for adequate mothering.

In unconscious phantasy the quality of internal objects which engenders trust is, in the first instance, beauty, later, probably only through the development of language, abstracted and dissected into its basic aspects, of goodness and strength. We shall see later how this primitive, pre-verbal significance of beauty in psychic reality is appropriated and counterfeited by the destructive part of the personality for its work of seduction. But even in a fortuitous way external reality is often dangerously misleading and, in a sense, disillusioning, when to it is applied expectations germane to that unity of beauty, goodness and strength which pertain in psychic reality. It provides an area of experience, accidental in essence, to which the term "traumatic" may be applied in its most strict sense. The prick of the thorn, the burn of the fire, the scratch of the cat, can lead to restrictions of ego development and to curtailment of optimism, directly traceable to this internal-external confusion, since these events have been apprehended as indistinguishable from betrayal by previously trusted objects. The clamping down on risk, the "never again" attitude, is its special mark on character formation.

It appears to be a function of the trust in good objects to modify sibling rivalry and the floods of anxiety upon which it is based. In comprehending psychic structure it is always important to remember that the various infantile parts of the self stand, at their highest state of integration, in the relationship of siblings one to another. But this capacity to share the good objects is absolutely dependent on the trust in the justice of good objects as a sub-category of their goodness. It is a pre-condition for intimacy without collusion between the siblings and this makes possible a companionship, in separation from good objects, which vastly increases the tolerance to the mental pains attendant on those situations.

This companionship by integration of infantile structures is coupled with another aspect of trust in good objects, and together they appear to determine the basic attitude to mental pain at infantile levels, largely unconscious in grown-ups. This second factor is the trust in the availability of good objects, namely that a call for help will be heard and answered. This factor plays an immense role in the technical requirements of the analytic setting for the carrying of the deepest infantile transference by an analyst, but it is too complex a subject to be dealt with here. It must be compounded of a belief, by the infant, that it is introjected and preserved by the parent (or analyst), with a trust in the goodness of the object in terms of its readiness for sacrifice, particularly to sacrifice its pleasures to the needs of the infant. The failure of development of this aspect of trust, in infants of very sensuous and depressive make-up, seems to play a large part, for instance, in setting autistic mechanisms in motion.

It must be kept in mind that when we spoke of the *dramatis personae* of the primal scene, we were speaking schematically for the sake of evolving a working classification of sexual states of mind. This in no way reflects a steady state in the organisation of the personality which is in fact always, to some extent, in flux. There is an ebb and flow of splitting and reintegration, probably occurring simultaneously at different levels of the mind. Just as the dream or dreams we may study in a particular analytic session are only those few of the nights' continuum that have been hooked into remembrance in waking, so also our analysis of them penetrates the meaning only at that level which is particularly active in the transference at the moment. Our analytic method follows a thread through its ramifications and connections, much as the selective

silver stains with which Freud as a young man worked in his neuro-
anatomy researches enabled him to follow the ramifications and
connections of a particular neurone.

This is extremely important in understanding psychic structure,
especially so when we approach the clinical manifestations of
disordered sexual states and find evidence even in the most healthy
minds of loculated pathology. These loculations are connected with
splitting processes and with the vulnerability of good parts of the
infantile organisation to be fragmented by the divide-and-conquer
techniques of the destructive part of the personality. However,
experience suggests that these splitting processes are not operative in
relation to the destructive part, which tends to retain a unity of
structure and to be strongly defended against being drawn into the
sphere of good objects. In order not to become time-bound and
subject to persecutory and depressive anxieties, it employs different
techniques from those which we ordinarily designate as mechanisms
of defence. They appear in relatively pure culture in the tricks of
interpersonal relations (not of object relations, for they are highly
narcissistic in their organisation) of psychopaths; the liar, cheat,
poseur, confidence man, tramp, professional gambler, dope pusher,
committed pervert, dedicated anarchist. These all express one or
other of the fundamental techniques of attack on the integration of
the idealised family which the destructive part employs.

The fundamental method, of course, is the creation of confusion.
The basic aim is the restoration of the chaos from which the good
parts of the self will crave release at any cost, even of the abandonment of the real world, meaning external *and* psychic reality, in
favour of the "brave new world" of delusion formation and
schizophrenia. This latter corresponds to Freud's "reconstruction
phase" of that terrible illness from which, perhaps, no personality
totally escapes. Regression, in its structural sense as well as in its
earlier meaning of regression of the libido, is guided by the destructive part, by the creation, or really the recreation, of the confusional
states which had been traversed one by one, laboriously, during
development under the guidance of good internal and external
objects. First trust is loosened by aggravation of depressive
anxieties through jealousy until they are difficult to distinguish from
persecutions. Then sensuality is catered for by zonal confusions
until infantile polymorphism and perversity are indistinguishable.
Thirdly the retreat from the confines of time and identity are fostered
by the confusing of inside and outside through projective identification; manic denial of psychic reality is then asserted and the stage is
set for the fifth and final attack, on the differentiation of good and
bad by means of which "freedom is slavery" and "hate is love" usher

in the world of "Big Brother". The victim of regression need then only cease to struggle, abandon himself to the voluptuousness of despair and greet the new world of delusion with "tears of gratitude".

The destructive part of the self then presents itself to suffering good parts first as protector from pain, second as servant to its sensuality and vanity, and only covertly—in the face of resistance to regression —as the brute, the torturer. But the hint of violence always exists in its approach, and regression never would go very far without it, so homesick is the wandererer.

It can be of great clinical value to differentiate the perverse sexual states of mind according to these five steps of the regressive process. In order for infantile polymorphous sexuality to be clung to, the differentiation of depressive and persecutory mental pain must be maintained, at the threshold of the depressive position. Within the infantile polymorphous area, the zonal confusions are based on ignorance and inadequate introjective identification: that is inadequate commitment to these identifications. They are zonal hypotheses which must be tested for lack of guidance, through identification. But the zonal confusions of perversity are no longer hypotheses. They are acted upon as theories arrogantly asserted. The crucial opting for massive projective identification which opens the way to psychosis is thus different from infantile polymorphous experimentation with it. Correspondingly, neurotic perversity may take masochistic or sadistic form almost fortuitously, depending on external influences, and may alternate in accordance with external opportunities. But psychotic perversity either denies psychic reality manically and enters an oscillating relation to internal figures in projective identification, as in cyclothymia, or abandons psychic reality en route to the insanities. The reversal of good and bad is the final step then to despair and delusional system-formation.

This carries us to the point where we may consider some of the therapeutic implications of this way of viewing perverse sexual states of mind and their place in the structure of mental disturbance. It is a view that is unequivocally committed to a conception of evil and views the bad infantile part of the personality, in its fluctuating state of fusion with split off "bad" parts of the objects, in the light of Milton's Prince of Darkness who would rather rule in hell than serve in heaven. Its envious competitiveness with idealised objects causes it to simulate their qualities of beauty, goodness and strength in ways calculated to dazzle the imagination of the good infantile structures. Through masturbatory activity it can excite states of omnipotence in relation to internal objects. By confusion of internal and external reality it can assert this omnipotence in the outside world as well, and, by careful selection of situations, even simulate it. But probably its most powerful tool for influencing the good infantile parts, suffering as they do from their ignorance, is through its assertion of omniscience. This is a technique which, for its effect, plays upon poverty of imagination to confine the boundaries of possible knowledge on the one hand, and upon the sluggishness of thinking to foster logical fallacy. The combination of the two make for the common sense of bigotry, the "where-there's-smoke-there's-fire" mentality. This is an area of understanding to which Wilfred Bion and Roger Money-Kyrle have made outstanding contributions to our therapeutic equipment.

The therapeutic implication, in its broadest sense, is that psycho-analysis is a rescue operation and cannot be undertaken in safety. At its extreme is the maelstrom of schizophrenia and perhaps none of us really dares to enter its vortex. The countertransference pitfalls of a method of rescue are too complex for us to enter upon here, but a systematic investigation, which premature death interrupted, was commenced by Heinrik Racker and can be found in his book, "Transference and Countertransference". The issue, of whether psycho-analysis, as a therapy, is a method to help the patient investigate his unconscious or is a method by which an analyst rescues the lost children of a patient's personality—or both at different times—is perhaps the great point of cleavage in the psycho-analytic movement.

Before closing this chapter, a word must be said about the old descriptive terminology. Of the many words employed, only "sadistic" and "masochistic" find a place in a psycho-analytical classification of states of mind. The rest, homosexual, heterosexual, transvestite, fellatio, fetishism, lesbian, etc., must be held as purely descriptive in relation to sexual acts. Our roster of metapsychogical terms would be restricted to the following: active-passive, male-female, zonal delineations, good-bad, inside-outside, external-internal, sadistic-masochistic, neurotic-psychotic, adult-infantile. For instance the state of mind underlying an act descriptively homosexual in a man might be found to be: passive feminine vaginal infantile. It would thus be an act of immature infantile polymorphism, as so much early adolescent so-called homosexuality, say in all-male environments, surely is.

CHAPTER 14

Terror, Persecution and Dread*

THIS chapter is intended as a contribution to the exploration of the paranoid-schizoid position in object relations, as defined by Melanie Klein. It is the result of analytic work employing the deeper understanding of personality made possible by her discoveries of the role of splitting processes in the formation of psychic structure and the mechanism of projective identification in the dynamics of object relations.

A spectrum of psychic pains is subsumed under the category of paranoid anxieties, the study of which has been begun in detail by other authors, *e.g.* confusion by Rosenfeld, catastrophic anxiety by Segal and Bion, nameless dread by Bion. Less well-defined terms such as hopelessness, despair, helplessness, must also be dealt with, but this paper is limited to three: terror, persecution, and dread. I will attempt to define these mental pains metapsychologically and to show their place and interaction in the analytical process, employing a case presentation to show them at work.

Case Material

Although this cultured and intelligent man in his late thirties entered analysis because of somatic symptoms, extensive character pathology was soon revealed. Early in the analysis the narcissistic organisation expressed itself clearly in the following dream: *He was walking uphill on a lonely woodland track and saw another man about his age, a former business client of very paranoid disposition, ahead of him. When the track divided, instead of going to the right as he had intended, he followed the other man, going down on to a beach which he recognised as belonging to the village where he had been born (and from which he had departed at the age of six months when his parents emigrated). On the beach he listened with admiration as the other man declaimed at length about his income and importance, how even on holiday he had to keep in constant touch with his office, as they could do nothing without his advice.*

As this part of his infantile structure showed up several times in

* Read to the International Congress of Psycho-analysis, Copenhagen, 1967, and published in the Int. J. Psa., 49, 1968.

dreams as a fox, having a reference to a childhood picture story book, it came to be known as his "foxy" part and could be seen to be the source of several types of mental content and phenomena. It produced a constant punning and caricaturing of other people's words (including analytic interpretations); elaborated an endless stream of cleverly screened pornographic limericks; supplied a relentless line of cynical and snobbish argument; and carried on a visual and auditory scrutiny of his environment just outside consciousness. This latter produced a series of dreams in the transference which indicated a most intimidating monitoring of the analyst's technique and way of life. For instance, he knew that I had a colleague who lived in a road that he regularly drove along on his way to analysis. On the night after I had borrowed this colleague's car, and despite my having taken the precaution of parking it around the corner, the patient dreamed that my colleague had a hole, about the size of a car, in the road before his house. The patient had not consciously, however, either seen the borrowed car, noted the absence of my usual one, nor noted the vacancy in front of the colleague's house.

The know-it-all quality of this "foxy" part and its hold over other infantile structures did not, however, yield in the slightest to the analytic investigation. Rather it seemed paradoxically to strengthen its hold as a result of two revelations, both of which were reconstructed from the dreams before they were admitted by the patient. The first of these was a secret sado-masochistic masturbatory perversion and the second was a terror of fire. The paradoxical strengthening of the symptoms had a peculiarly defiant quality. He asserted that his perversion was the only pleasure in his life and sustained him from suicide. The terror of fire was claimed as absolutely rational on the one hand, and sanctified by trauma during the war on the other. He did not in the least acknowledge that these two arguments were mutually exclusive.

A further area of psycho-pathology which resisted investigation was his relationship to his ageing mother, whose development of a chronic ailment had been shortly followed by the somatic symptoms which led the patient to analysis. While his relation to her had been cool and even contemptuous from late adolescence, her illness was extremely persecuting to him. He appropriated from his siblings, in a slavish custodial manner, the supervision of the mother's health, financial problems and household affairs, consciously motivated by devotion to his long-deceased father, as if charged by him exclusively with the mother's care. The persecutory element was linked with the perversion, whose secret pleasures were felt as the oasis in a desert of deprivation spitefully imposed by the ailing mother out of her own incapacity for pleasure. The constellation had arisen slowly when it had become clear with the passage of years that his mother would not re-marry. It had replaced the tyrannical and jealously possessive demeanour toward her which characterised the years immediately following his father's death. The turning point had occurred on the occasion of his mother's flat being considerably damaged, though not beyond repair, by incendiary bombs. At the time he had been able to fight the fire with courage, but shortly thereafter developed his terror of fire and would rush from the house at the hint of a raid to sleep in a nearby ditch, leaving his mother alone in the undamaged part.

In the following years the perversion crystallised a fixed pattern: dressed in a chauffeur's uniform, sitting on the inner tube of a car tyre, holding a glass of whisky, he would masturbate genitally and anally. The expulsive significance of the orgasm was indicated in analysis in a dream in which, *sitting on the tube over a well, he defaecated and then threw his clothes down the well*. The prehistory of the perversion was of interest and could be accurately dated to an incident in which his father had needed to remove, repair, blow up, and replace a punctured tyre of the family car during an outing, the spare being missing. The little boy was overwhelmed with sexual excitement watching his father and thereafter developed several symptoms and secret activities. One of these was the habit of sucking on the dirty tyres of his bicycle. The other was an exciting game of letting the air out of a bicycle tyre, waiting then until a policeman would come along, attempting to blow it up with his mouth as the policeman watched. But he also developed a fear of riding in the family car which was too sternly dealt with.

In order to comprehend the anxieties which the analysis found to underlie the perversion and the character pathology, another factor must be noted; again a mixture of trauma and fate. The patient was the youngest child and only boy. A particular traumatic incident of early childhood had assumed a screen memory function. When he was five, probably, after being united with his mother following her protracted illness which had entirely altered the family plans for the future, he was on a country stroll with his nanny and came upon a dead infant, left under a hedge. This incident became fixedly bound in his mind to his own naughty habit; when given lunch in the garden he would always secretly throw away into the hedge the detested cold fatty meat.

For the first three years of his analysis, which was occupied largely with his tendencies to massive projective indentification and "pseudo-maturity", this constellation of perversion, character pathology and symptoms were kept from analysis by acting-out in which his "foxy" part was split off into a close business associate by whom he felt dominated. But as this lessened and his own "foxiness" became more conscious and clearly manifest in the transference, two things happened. First of all there took shape a new hopefulness about the possibility of being released through analysis from his constricted life. Consequently, with the acceptance of some measure of dependence on the analytic process, his conscious co-operation became divested of its lacunae of secretiveness. Secondly his attitude toward mental pain altered, so that his cowardice, earlier paraded as a cynical self-interest and snobbery, was allowed a central place as object of analytic investigation.

In the following years, the fourth and fifth years of analysis, the material made possible a dissection of his persecutory anxieties. Progress toward a deeper infantile dependence (on the analytic breast as an introjective object) could commence: the threshold of the depressive position was reached in the analytic process.

As the work of the two months prior to the fifth Christmas break and the one month after seem so crucial and clear, I will try to describe them in some detail.

The struggle to abandon the perversion could be seen clearly as a struggle to put his faith in the analysis and the analytic parents. He dreamed that *he was at at school taking a Latin exam. He thought it might be a trick question, but decided to decline the noun in the straightforward manner of "mensa"* (a pun on Meltzer). Or he dreamed *he was visiting his old school and had to decide whether to drive with the chauffeur and boys or to accompany the pleasant mistress* (to choose between "foxy" and analysis).

The uncertainty seemed to relate to doubts about the strength, not the goodness or sincerity, of the analytic parents. The night after I had had a tiny cut over one eye, which the patient had not consciously noticed, he dreamed that *he was complaining to the analyst about a cut over one eye he himself had received in a plane crash and that he might have been killed due to the pilot's carelessness.* The intensity of the dependence was apparent.

But as his confidence grew, so did his identification with a capable and courageous "daddy". This was manifest in dreams and behavior in which he confronted situations he had always cowered from, as well as persons who represented the "foxy" and "vixen" aspects of his own infantile structure. In one dream *he protected his son's guinea-pig from a weasel;* in another *he chased away hoodlums assaulting an old man. But when confronted in a dream with a former friend who had developed a paranoid breakdown, the best he could do was to hide in the nursery.* In reality when this man had paid him an unexpected visit, he could not help placating him when he demanded that my patient join in a bizarre prayer to "the Spirit". This, we knew, touched terribly closely on his terror of fire and, as he now revealed, of ghosts, or spirits. We had already seen many dreams in which spirit lamps caught fire. It became clear also that his dislike of swimming was in fact a terror of deep water, not from fear of drowning but a terror of monsters seizing him from below. Material also indicated that this constellation played a part in his impotence and aversion to the female genital.

It was very close to Christmas; his mother seemed to be losing ground and his inner trust in the vitality of good objects seemed to collapse as the theme of the "dead baby" once more took hold. He was dreaming again *of a dead octopus on the front step, of worms in the lawn, of a dead crab under a rock*. He had an experience of terror one morning when some flour fell from a bread roll as he drew it from the oven, flaring in the gas fire. He lay in paralysed terror one night when a sound from his daughter's bedroom was construed as an explosion of the TV machine. Some nights later he was seized by a paralysing terror at sounds downstairs felt to be an insane intruder. His dreams reflected the renewed hopelessness. *The Nazis were counter-attacking in England* or *Brighton was being bombed*.

However in fact he felt better when awake in the holiday and noted gains in his vigour and courage. *He was terribly griefstricken* in a dream in which *his mother had died and her belongings were being stored. But the couch which was being carried away was the analytic couch*. He understood by himself how clearly linked now were the analysis, his mother and his internal good objects. In a later dream *he was scolded by a woman for starting a fire in the stove with his methylated spirit lamp. She ordered him to stay back saying that she'd called the fire brigade and in the meantime the automatic spray-pipe would keep things under control*. In a word, his internal mother forbade his manic reparativeness, telling him that her internal penis would suffice until the "daddy" arrived.

By this time the three different qualities of anxiety—persecution, dread and terror—were very distinct in his conscious experience. This was of course to some extent due to alteration in the economics of anxiety in that he was more depressed than persecuted by damaged objects, less cowardly toward bad parts of himself and the dreaded persons representing them, and more aware that the terror situations had a basis in psychic reality which could be both comprehended and corrected. Attention in the work could now be turned to the problem of the recurrent destruction and restoration of the internal mother's babies and its transference manifestations in regard to the analyst's children: publications and interpretations—brain children. This work involved the prevention of the destructive attacks (his masturbation attacks, as in the perversion) by the patient taking greater responsibility for psychic reality. But true reparation also was made possible by the relinquishment of the acting out of his manic reparativeness, so epitomised in his snobbish contempt for manual work and idealisation of intellectual pursuits. One such episode was the following. After dreaming that *he chased a wasp from the family car*, he developed an episode of abdominal pain, which lasted several days. It resolved after a dream in which *his father was repairing the inner tube of a tyre, though the patient half-hoped that the butt of the nail had been left in the tyre*. After the following session in which his critical and competitive attitude toward the analytic-daddy was scrutinised, he dreamed that *a terrible noise coming from a gap in the hedge terrified him, until a little terrier dog appeared. But when it ran ahead of him to his mother's house, it seemed to turn into his father's boxer dog.*

In the working through of this problem during the following year, many episodes occurred, clustering about the separations, of attacks on the mother's internal babies in masturbatory or acted-out forms. His various forms of manic reparation were reduced and the resolution of his oedipal conflict instituted. The attacks of terror disappeared and the residual clinging to the perversion was finally abandoned.

Discussion of Clinical Material

The material demonstrates how the systematic analysis of the transference made it possible to see the different qualities of the patient's anxieties and the organisation of his narcissism as a defensive structure. He was *terrified* of the "dead-babies", the "fire-bomb" babies, the ghostly "burning-flour-off-the-bap" babies. He was persecuted by his damaged objects—his dead father, his impaired mother, his defective analyst—by whom he was deprived of pleasure, of leisure, of money, of comfort; for whom he had to work, to be respectable, to earn a living, to know about a world of economics, health, morality and politics in which he felt no interest. He *dreaded* and was submitted to the tyranny of his "foxy" part, which demanded his participation in his perversion long after it had ceased to be his oasis of secret pleasure. This destructive part prevented him from admiring or respecting anyone by its slander, its omniscient propaganda. It kept him in a state of impotence by its denigration of the female genital, while it threatened him with homosexual desires by presenting penises as delicious suckable nipples. But, above all, "foxy" offered him protection from the terror of the dead babies—or so it claimed. Only in the transference, as in the dream of the little-dog-in-the-hedge, did he come to realise that his "foxy" part had never protected him, that in fact he had been protected all along by an external good object, fundamentally his mother; in the transference by the analyst, psychoanalysis, the analytic breast, with its power to project, despite his enfeebled introjective power, a reparative vitality into his inner world—just as his mother had nourished the recalcitrant little boy who secretly threw the cold meat into the hedge. The series of dreams of live and dead babies (the dead crab, the dead octopus, the terrifying gap-in-the-hedge, etc.) gradually showed him the real nature of his dependence and enabled him to rebel against his tyrant, "foxy", as seen in the dreams such as that of the weasel, or the assault on the old man. Submission to "foxy" and the perversion had yielded to the acknowledgement of absolute dependence at infantile levels on his primal good objects in psychic reality.

Only with this step forward did an amelioration of his persecution by damaged objects begin to give way to depressive concern for them, in dreams, in the transference, in his relations to his mother. Where despair had yielded to hopelessness, hope now arose.

Theoretical Discussion and Summary

Terror is a paranoid anxiety whose essential quality, paralysis, leaves no avenue of action. The object of terror (being in unconscious phantasy dead objects) cannot even be fled from with success. But in psychic reality the vitality of an object, of which it may be robbed, can also be returned to it, as the soul to the body in theological terms. This can only be accomplished by the reparative capacity of the internal parents and their creative coitus.

When dependence on the reparative capacity of the internal objects is prevented by oedipal jealousy and/or destructive envy, this restoration cannot occur during the course of sleep and dreaming. Only an object in external reality, which bears the transference significance of the mother's breast at infantile levels, can accomplish the task. This may be undertaken innumerable times without being acknowledged, if the infantile dependence is blocked by the denigrating activity of envy or the obstinacy born of intolerance to separation.

Where dependence on internal good objects is rendered infeasible by damaging masturbatory attacks and where dependence on a good external object is unavailable or not acknowledged, the addictive relationship to a bad part of the self, the submission to tyranny, takes place. An illusion of safety is promulgated by the omniscience of the destructive part and perpetuated by the sense of omnipotence generated by the perversion or addictive activity involved. The tyrannical, addictive bad part is *dreaded*. It is important to note that, while the tyrant may behave in a way that has a resemblance to a persecutor, especially if any sign of rebellion is at hand, the essential hold over the submissive part of the self is by way of the dread of loss of protection against terror. I have come to the conclusion that intolerance of depressive anxieties alone will not produce the addictive constellation of submission to the tyrant. Where a dread of loss of an addictive relation to a tyrant is found in psychic structure, the problem of terror will be found at its core, as the force behind the dread and the submission.

Until such a narcissistic organisation is dismantled and a rebellion against the tyranny of the bad part is mounted, progress into the threshhold of the depressive position is impossible. Furthermore, until this occurs, factors in psychopathology such as intolerance of separation, or of depressive pain, or cowardice in the face of persecution, cannot be accurately estimated. The dread felt in relation to the tyrant is fundamentally a dread of loss of the illusory protection against the terror and may be seen to appear especially at times when rebellion has been undertaken in alliance with good objects which are then felt to be inadequate or unavailable, as during analytic holiday breaks.

CHAPTER 15

The Origins of the Fetishistic Plaything of Sexual Perversions*

As with the differentiation between "depressive" as an adjective denoting a quality of mental pain (depressive anxieties) and as a term denoting an organisation of mental pathology (depressive illness), so we must distinguish the uses of the term "perverse" in regard to sexuality. I wish to use it to indicate those erotic phantasies or activities in which the inflicting of mental or physical suffering or injury is central to the excitement—*perverse sexuality*. But I also wish to indicate an organisation of such tendencies into a structural category of clinical psychopathological symptoms, *sexual perversion*. It is doubtful whether one would wish to use the term to describe a person as a "pervert" except as a shorthand notation.

In the use of the term to denote a type of sexuality we are emphasising the impulses and its consequent phantasy and activity, neglecting the other metapsychological areas which contribute to the final manifestation. But in speaking of "perversion", as a type of symptom, we are including all four metapsychological areas. The complexity of the problem was acknowledged by Freud in "A Child is Being Beaten" and "The Economic Problem of Masochism" in relation to structure (the role of identification) and economics. But the category of object choice was not specifically modified beyond the statement of the "Three Essays". I now wish to examine the possibility that the categories of narcissism versus object-relations do not adequately account for the nature of the object of excitement in perversions nor for the peculiar quality of the excitement and socialisation observed in these symptoms.

What appears below makes an approach that has a fundamental resemblance to that made by Donald Winnicott in his formulations of "transitional objects" and the use made of this concept by Masud Khan in his study of perversion. Those familiar with this work will immediately recognise that what we have formulated here raises questions regarding the differentiation good-bad, and the distinction between mock-reparative activity and the state of mind of true reparation. True reparative activity itself is a process resulting from

* Read to the British Psycho-analytical Society, 4th June 1969.

introjective identification with the reparative activities (coitus) of the internal objects. This will be discussed at greater length later on.

The approach is also very closely linked to that of Gillespie. He writes of a flagellant: "By 'object' I do not mean the female partners of his flagellations, who were of little significance to him as people, but only as fellow enthusiasts and necessary to the execution of his phantasies; these were always in some degree spoiled by the imperfections of reality. No, the real object seemed to be the instrument of whipping and his attitude to whips was very similar to that of a fetishist to his fetish". Gillespie described the role of splitting of self and object in the formation of the personality structure of the pervert. I plan to bring this thesis into relation to a special type of splitting in the formation of these special objects, which I have called "fetishistic playthings", in order to broaden the concept "fetish".

The thesis I wish to present is that the objects of sexual excitement about which perversions crystallise are "dismantled objects", as distinct from part-objects. This "dismantled object" may be the same as Winnicott's "transitional object", but, as he traces his definition in terms of a reconstruction of childhood rather than by drawing directly upon the phenomenology of the consulting room, this equation is not certain. The definition I am using here of "dismantled object" is drawn from psycho-analytical treatment of children who have suffered from early infantile autism. In substance our findings indicate that the most primitive working of obsessional mechanisms (omnipotent control over, and separation of, objects) dismantles objects by a very careful method which makes possible immediate reconstitution of the original object when desired. In this respect they differ from the splitting processes described by Melanie Klein, which employ sadisitc impulses to cleave objects, thereby doing a certain amount of violence and damage. The objects cleft by splitting processes can only be repaired with difficulty, as manifest by certain aspects of the pains of the depressive position.

The method of dismantling objects employs the differentiation of the senses, or the dissolution of "common sense" in Bion's terms (or "consensual validation", in Sullivan's). It appears to be accomplished by selective attention to the unisensual qualities of a diversity of external objects. But this dismantling of a common sense object into a host of unisensual ones seems to preclude introjection and allows only for apprehension of an immediate sensual event. I hesitate to use the word "experience" as I wish to reserve that for relationship events which can be introjected, and thus become available for memory. Consequently I suspect that the phenomenon of "satisfaction" is also precluded in the dismantling of objects and that an insatiability indistinguishable descriptively from greed results.

A further difficulty in this mode of degradation of objects reveals the essential failure of the defence when it is mounted against depressive anxieties, as we shall see in the clinical material to follow. This difficulty resides in the degradation of the emotionality from love to sensuality. While the initial dismantling may have been undertaken out of concern for the safety of the object and with an eye to its future reconstitution, once it has been reduced to a unisensual assortment, the sum-of-the-parts no longer equals the whole in value, exactly as in the case of ordinary splitting into part-objects. These dismantled objects are "devalued" (as distinct from "denigrated" as a specific form of anal attack on an object) and not worth protecting from further sadistic attack by bad parts of the self.

Clinical Material

A patient who came to analysis for two reasons, lack of creativity in his scientific work and persistence of a schoolboy perversion, soon realised their interaction with one another, or rather their negative relationship. It became clear that his scientific work lacked passion because he was a musician *manqué*, just as his sexual relation with his wife was lacking due to his secret perversion. History suggested a single origin. His formal musical studies, stimulated by his mother's singing and playing, had begun at an early age when, along with a cousin, he had been evacuated from the danger of bombing. During this six months there grew up between the two boys, approximately the same age, a game of spanking bottoms which crystallised for my patient into the homosexual activity of his schooldays and the perversion of his adult life. Its relation to waiting, or having "time on his hands" was absolutely clear. It consequently erupted at week-ends and holidays in the analysis and led him into wanderings that were both corrupting and dangerous. He dreamed: *that he was flirting with a schoolboy in the ploughed field behind the ugly backside of a building which he knew to have a beautiful Georgian facade.* He commented that the ploughing was like lines of magnetic force and we came to refer to this phenomenon as the "field of forces behind mummy's backside". This division between front and back of his object was very important to his resentment, for he was unable, clearly, to distinguish between the ugliness of his thoughts and feelings and the qualities of his object.

But this problem of resentment of separation, with its oedipal quality, was further complicated by a problem of mourning, for his father had died while my patient was in early puberty, before his oedipal coolness had permitted recovery of the earlier admiration and feminine attachment. The Easter break in analysis approximated to the anniversary of the death and threw up material which showed the part played by defence against mourning and depressive pain in the persistence of the perversion. He dreamed: *he was with his little daughter and childhood nanny, Trude, waiting for an Easter oratorio. Everyone except himself "goggled" when Jackie Kennedy and Marlene Dietrich entered. But when the music started he seemed to be in a side corridor, unable to see, now without Trude. Then he seemed to be going up a hillside, away from the town, the music in the distance, holding his daughter's hand, as if fleeing from the Cities of the Plain. And finally he was without his daughter, in a room with a TV of the oratorio, and seated behind him was a famous composer and his homosexual paramour.*

I select this dream because it shows very clearly the step by step process of degradation of his object, from the orchestra breasts to his own composer-homosexual buttocks.

Step I: He is waiting for the feed in an integrated state of bisexuality (with his little-girl-self-daughter) and in a truthful (Trude) relationship to mother. We knew that Trude's name and her watchful eyes had this meaning. For instance in the "field-of-forces" dream, he retreated with the schoolboy to a tunnel lest Trude might see them.

Step II: When the sexual beauty of the breasts (Jackie and Marlene) is exposed to others' "goggling" he dismantles his visual relation by looking away, so that:

Step III: By the time the music (feed) has commenced he has become secretive (no longer with Trude; in a corridor as in the tunnel of the "field-of-forces" dream).

Step IV: In which the source of the music is put behind him (the Cities of the Plain) and he is holding on to his bottom as a part of himself (his little Lot's-wife-daughter-bottom). A *volte face* now produces:

Step V: In which the little-girl bottom, changed to the pillar-of-salt-TV-screen (bottle), is before him and behind him are his homosexual composer-buttocks.

The elements I wish to stress are the dismantling of the visual from the auditory apprehension of the object and abandonment of the truth. By these two processes the stage is set for a regression to narcissism, graphically represented in the dream as the leaving of the concert hall and even the city where it was located. But the special perverse aspect of the narcissism, the Sodom and Gomorrah aspects, were not immediately evident, until it became clear that a very special relation to his cousin existed in respect of music. Both had been very musical and while listening they would exchange glances that implied a unity of mind which, he complained, he had never felt with his wife.

This idealised "unity of mind" was in fact conspiratorial in significance, namely that, although they had seemed such good boys on the surface, they had a secret from the grown-ups, their bottom paddling. Some months later in the analysis, when a prolonged abstinence from the perversion had been accompanied by a more potent and emotional relation to his wife, he was surprised to find the bottom-spanking behaviour erupting with her, and not too well received. At that time he dreamed, before a weekend, that *he was holding on to the back of Lady Chichester's paddle-steamer and being towed upstream.* It now became clear that the separation from the analytic parents during the "evacuation" week-end was being attributed to their having a honeymoon trip around the world. It was thus being utilised to deny the fear of the possible death of the parents. This same device must have been used in childhood and later on to deny the mother's separation from the father by virtue of his death.

What I am suggesting is that the defence against depressive anxiety through denial of danger to the parents had aggravated the oedipal resentment and wish to punish them for their sexuality. But by dismantling the object and abandoning concern for the truth, the whole conflict was changed into a secret, perverse game, homosexual only in the descriptive sense, fortuitously due to circumstance (evacuation with his cousin, later boarding school, etc.).

There was good reason to believe that the patient's talents and desires were very strongly musical, but that the integrative relations to the art had given way to this perverse one, in which the secret "unity-of-mind" with the cousin-composer-buttocks overrode the primary relation to the musician-mother (combined object).

Approximately six months later, this formulation of "dismantling" found a very convincing confirmation in a dream which showed very clearly the reassembly of the object. In the meanwhile a rather striking improvement had occurred in his relationship to his mother externally and in his feelings of love and desire toward his wife, much of which seemed to date from a dream that reversed that series of dreams which had culminated in the "field-of-forces-behind-mummy's-backside" dream. In this dream *he had watched with awe as his mother, naked, in the distance, was entering the waters of the sea. Her beauty quite overwhelmed him.* He associated this scene with representations in art of the Birth of Venus. In the meanwhile, the father person in his inner world, sometimes actually his father in fact, was appearing regularly in dreams and oedipal conflict was becoming rather high at week-ends and in expectation of the summer holiday. He dreamed that *he was standing with a man* (who in fact had recently written a book, his first, which had met with very high praise from a senior woman of that field) *named Taylor, looking down from a platform at the seated nude figure of Julie Felix* (a Canadian folk singer whom he had recently seen on the street and had thought rather disappointingly small and toothy. He also thought the analyst Canadian.). *She seemed to have been away some time to have a baby but was also about to be married. Taylor went down to greet her, and invited her to rise and stretch, which she did. The patient was both awed at her beauty and struck by the lack of lust in Taylor's friendly and admiring demeanour. She then seemed to be in a room, reclining by a fireplace clad in a most unusual transparent garment consisting of strings upon which* (*like scales*) *were arranged small elliptical pieces of thin gold which tinkled delightfully at every slight movement* (like Chinese glass pendants). *It seemed clear that this was her wedding dress, as if designed by Taylor.*

It became clear in further associations that the shape of the tiny pieces of gold was like the shape of the human eye, and that the strings were like the lines of the musical staff; hence the pun on "scales". The point that I wish to make is that the reassembly of the object in regard to the visual and auditory beauty is accomplished by the Taylor-daddy (also a pun) whose non-lustful relation to the mother's beauty enables the son, by identification, to overcome his own tendency to denigration of the breast (seeing Julie as disappointingly small and toothy when he undresses her with his eyes).

Only later in the analysis did we realise that the gustatory and olfactory relation to the mother's body had suffered a similar "dismantling". With their reassembly, oedipal rage and jealous possessiveness broke out in dreams in a manner most astonishing to the patient. For instance, he dreamed *that his wife and her friend were being tickled by the milkman. He flew into a rage, throwing the milkman about like a sack and pummelling his wife until he was quite exhausted.* This dream is undoubtedly at a part-object level: milkman penis-nipple, wife-and-friend breasts.

Discussion

In the foregoing material there is really nothing to suggest that we are dealing with phenomena related to fetishism, in the clinical descriptive sense. But clearly, what I am suggesting is that when we are able to trace the origins of the object-choice in perversions accurately we find a process indistinguishable from the formation of a fetish. I am therefore suggesting another aspect of the problem that arises in understanding the genesis of perverse symptoms (sexual perversions), differentiated from perverse sexuality as modes of phantasy and behaviour having their origins in the Id.

The crystallisation of a perversion is a highly complicated affair of ego and super-ego structure and relationship. In the Chapter on "Terror" I have traced the particular constellation of anxieties which predispose to the addictive type of narcissistic organisation that underlies the perversion. In this Chapter I am suggesting the particular role of object-choice, which I would now prefer to call "object-formation", that is brought about by a primitive type of obsessional mechanism, the "dismantling" of objects. In effect we are following Freud's suggestion that fetish-formation involves a splitting in the ego and I am showing that this is a very special type of splitting, different from that described later by Melanie Klein. By following this special form of splitting, or dismantling, we find that its application to perversions is more general than has been thought and that a type of object-formation, identical to fetish-formation, is ubiquitous in the perversions proper, that is, in the sado-masochistic game with which an addictive attachment can be formed. It is well-known that the addictive repetition binds both the most severe anxieties and the most violent perverse impulses. The findings put forward here help to account for the shallow and even silly type of excitement so characteristic of the perversion by demonstrating that it is brought about in a manner which reduces the projection-introjection of object relations not merely to a narcissistic organisation but to an autoerotic level of sensuality which precludes emotionality, memory or satisfaction. In recognising the fetish-like aspects of the object in perverse games, its utter replaceability by inanimate objects becomes clear as in the fetish proper or masturbatory devices of one sort or another. This element of auto-erotism accounts also for that quality of the socialised form of the perversions namely the mutuality, the "you-do-it-to-me-and-then-I'll-do-it-to-you" aspect.

CHAPTER 16

On The Distinction Ambisexual*: Bisexual

A COGENT case is often made for the contention that the disagreements amongst psycho-analysts are purely semantic, and that the true approximation of our language to our comprehension would cause this conflict to melt away like the dew beneath the rising sun. A more compelling position would tend to assume that our semantic confusions reflect quite accurately our conceptual ones. Under this thesis, further research in our understanding of mental phenomena would need to precede linguistic investigation.

It is probably the psycho-sexual area of psycho-analysis which best illustrates this dilemma, due to the two-fold origin of our technical vocabulary, half from psychiatry, based on description, half from metapsychology, based on interpretation. Systematic clarification of our language in respect of sexuality is one of the subsidiary aims of this volume, but one which can only be achieved semantically after conceptual clarification. This course has already been followed in several instances of differentiation: polymorphous from perverse; adult from infantile; descriptive "homosexual" from metapsychological "homosexual"; dependence from passivity. A further step must now be taken to distinguish between "bisexual" as a metapsychological and biological concept on the one hand, and "ambisexual" as a descriptive term in psychopathology to which we may hope to give metapsychological precision. In order to do this in depth, both terms must be given substance in relation to clinical phenomenology.

The genealogy of the term "bisexual", coming as it does from comparative anatomy, embryology and endocrinology, by way of Krafft-Ebbing, Havelock Ellis and the "Three Essays on Sexuality", rather dictates that we must use the term primarily in relation to the constitutional basis of sexual states of mind and consequent behaviour. But this does not preclude the possibility that we may wish to use it also descriptively in regard to sexual activities when we feel convinced that these acts are indeed a direct expression of this dual constitution. The burden of this chapter will be just this thesis, or rather its refutation. I intend to argue that bisexuality does not

* Ambisexuality: partial hermaphroditism, used particulary of behavioural conditions. Websters 3rd Int. Dictionary, 1961.

114

find direct expression in sexual acts in adult life; that the appearance of both heterosexual and homosexual acts, descriptively speaking, in the same individual after puberty is psychopathological; and that a separate term, "ambisexual", is required for its delineation.

Before undertaking this task, it is necessary to clear the field of a certain type of semantic debris relating to the concepts male:female, or rather masculine:feminine. We must set aside all historic, cultural or personal bias that would wish to appropriate specific traits of character or qualities of mind and fasten them preferentially to one or the other side of this dichotomy. Maleness and femaleness are highly complex concepts, differently faceted in meaning for different individuals and not to be bound to statistical ideas of normality, acculturation or adaptation. The meaning in the mind of each person is far more personal, related to the actual qualities of parental figures, as experienced in the early years, and too deeply rooted in the unconscious to be more than troubled, rather than influenced, by popular conceptions. No, we must use these terms in a manner firmly rooted in individuality by our clinical method, through which we claim to be able to distinguish different parts of the personality, one from the other.

If we are committed to this attitude, our position relative to Freud's extension of the concept of sexuality to cover the entire range of erotism is clear. We will consider the terms masculine and feminine to relate to those parts of the personality whose erotic identity is firmly bound to the differentiation of the sexes in its anatomical sense, genital organs and secondary sexual characteristics of the body, in keeping with the dictum that the ego is, in the first instance, a body ego. We will reserve judgement in regard to the individual of the sexual distribution, one might say, of such dichotomous mental characteristics as active:passive, dependent:receptive, muscular: sensual, hard:soft, big:small, intellectual:intuitive, defensive: aggressive, and so forth.

The first step in our argument will be dependent on an earlier Chapter of the book, in which it was undertaken to demonstrate that adult sexuality, metapsychologically speaking, derives from the introjective identification with the internal parental objects, and thus derives its polymorphous nature in a secondary way, not in a direct manner from the polymorphous and perverse disposition of the Id. It will be merely an extension of this conception to assert that, likewise, the bisexual nature of adult mental states have a secondary derivation. In so claiming we can be seen to adopt a position which is partly a matter of definition, namely that we have decided to call that structure of the personality which can be seen to arise from introjective identification with these figures "adult", as a distinction

from the descriptive term "grown up", and that we felt no embar-
rassment of contradiction whatever at having to recognise that these
structures arise very early, at least as early as the inception of the
latency period, long before the individual is grown up at all,
anatomically or culturally.

But it is not only a matter of definition, for in claiming that our
clinical method brings such structural differences clearly into view
we have laid the matter out for judgement by each individual
practitioner of psycho-analysis according to his own experience.
Consequently, what is asserted in this chapter regarding the psychopathological implications of ambisexual adjustment should be taken
only as a statement of the author's clinical experience. But it would
not be satisfactory to leave the matter there without some exposition
of the reasons why this experience seems to be in harmony with our
expectations. In order to do this lucidly, I will first present a brief
case history and some clinical material, on the basis of which the
matter can be debated.

Clinical Material

Two rather unfortunate intrusions upon the analytic process with a
married man in his forties came together during the third year of his
analysis, both throwing up some very interesting clinical material and
setting his resistance to working through upon the rock of factual
knowledge about the analyst. The first incident was that of reading
a rather hostile review of a book by Adrian Stokes containing some
particularly contemptuous remarks about a small section of the book
contributed by the analyst. The second, shortly after, involved seeing
the analyst at the theatre with a woman assumed, correctly, to be his
wife.

These events appeared at first to hasten a process that was already
under way, namely of bringing together the internal parents whose
separation in latency had been rigidly fixed by the sudden death of
the father when the boy was verging on puberty. The consequence
at that time had been both an inadequate mourning and the
crystallisation of perverse masturbatory phantasies centering on the
much-bruited homosexual inclinations of one of the masters at his
boarding school. His sexuality in adolescence was marked by a
confusion between male and female physical attributes in the bodies
and personalities of his objects of affection, but this sorted itself out
in two interconnecting directions. In the first place his sexual
preference turned quite unequivocally toward women, but his sexual
potency, or rather his ability to perform the sexual act with a woman,

was heavily dependent on secret masturbatory phantasies involving kissing young boys and beating their buttocks.

The intensification of the oedipal conflict took several forms at the same time. In his dreams there was mounting evidence of a parental intercourse going on somewhere, in the next room, the next garden, or a new organ was being installed in the old church, or the roof was being repaired on the old cattle shed so that it could be used for calves once more. In his waking life he became somewhat depressed and despondent about his poor progress, in life, in the analysis, in his technical mastery of his field of art. He felt rather envious of junior members of his profession, eyed with suspicion the evidences that houses were to be built in an open space near his home, was disturbed at night and unable to sleep at times due to a high-pitched sound which seemed to threaten an explosion or fire. At the same time his sexual relations with his wife fell away to nil and his preoccupation with boys took him wandering in the late afternoons, following the analytical sessions, looking at schoolboys' bottoms. He became somewhat jealous of his wife's relations with her elderly piano teacher and had dreams of possessiveness toward his little girl. Finally despite great feelings of guilt he began to see the young man with whom he had had homosexual activities prior to meeting his wife and felt in great danger of resuming the ambisexual promiscuity which had lasted some years from art school to his engagement.

In this context he produced a dream of great subtlety which he felt to be very important but could not say why. He withheld it for a session for no apparent reason, relating it in the next. In the dream *two friends came unexpectedly into his studio, one a current friend, Ralph, to tell him of his recent appointment to a university post, the other an old friend, Mario, bringing him a flask of Italian wine. He was surprised to see them together, for he had not even realised that they knew one another. Furthermore, Mario was dressed in the garb of the priesthood which he had years earlier abandoned to become a "continental pan-intellectual". The patient felt hard pressed to appear pleased with his one friend's success, due to envy, and with the other's gift. as it was not to his taste. He comforted himself with the thought that Ralph was a bachelor (not in fact true) and would have to live in college, as he put Mario's gift on the shelf.*

The patient, on waking, had recognised himself the main features of the dream, that it referred to the two intrusions, the two couples, Stokes: analyst and analyst: wife, which had come unexpectedly into his life. He further could see that Ralph being pictured as a bachelor living in college referred to the unmarried master at school whose supposed homosexual interests had so preoccupied the patient. At a deeper, part-object level Ralph and Mario represent two objects equated in confusion, that is the nipple-penis which is interested in the little boy's mouth and bottom and becomes the homosexual penis when it leaves the breast (puts off the garb of the priesthood). But in the dream the penis and breast (Mario back in the garb) are united as a combined object, represented as Ralph's new appointment, bringing the analytic present in touch with the infantile past represented by the generous Mario bringing intoxicating drink.

Of course, to say that such a dream is one of great subtlety may seem only a way of praising the subtlety of the analyst, but I mean to stress the subtle ways in which the ill-will, denigration, reduction to part-object status, and ingratitude, operate, so as not to interfere with the patient's self-image in its idealised aspects—his own friendliness, generosity, gratitude and honesty. The use of confusion as a defence is clearly indicated in the treatment of Mario, as the nipple-penis which is put back into the priestly garb of the breast as a form of ridicule, implying a loss of intellect and potency as compared with the "continental *Pan*-intellectual". The next step of begrudging the union of penis and breast to form a combined object makes of them a casual assortment, an odd-couple, Ralph and Mario, whose homosexuality is implied.

The other important point about a dream of this sort is that it presents so perfectly a plan of social action, a view of the world, a set of social values and code of conduct, that one would be inclined to say that its externalisation in action could never be identified as acting out in the specific and technical sense. It raises a problem concerning our understanding of the term "character". The idea of "character analysis" proper versus analysis of character "symptoms" would seem to pose a juxtaposition which only confuses matters. But as always what creates the confusion is the impingement of metapsychological insights upon descriptive categories. Descriptively the homosexual activities would be thought of as symptoms, and our assignment of psychopathological significance to it would be on the basis of social prejudices. In rebellion against this stigmatisation, the ambisexual individual will seek·to claim the converse, namely a special and elite release from social prejudice and inhibition by use of the term "bisexual".

Into this political sexual arena only a different point of view, based on different data and different criteria, can bring a détente, and eventual order. By penetrating into the depths, to gain a clear view of the structure of the self and the qualities of the objects, in addition to the more usual recognition of mechanisms, psycho-analysis can make a different type of statement, free from moral judgment and social censure. To say, therefore, "In *my* experience such-and-such", we are able to mean exactly that, a statement of limited experience inviting others to examine their own, rather than a formula for crushing opposition by the weight of authority, implying, "In *our* vast experience . . .".

Accordingly, in my experience, in treatment and supervision, ambisexual activities have always turned out to have the general structure illustrated by the clinical material presented here. In the first instance it becomes clear in the analysis that adult and infantile sexuality are very poorly differentiated. Next, the patient's defensive and eventually defiant attitude about the homosexual activities reveals a heavy defensive commitment. Eventually, the pseudo-potency of the heterosexual adjustment will become clear and the addictive aspect of the homosexual one is yielded to analytic inquiry. A period of heterosexual impotence may supervene, and indeed it can last very long if the sexual partner is not demanding or a stable heterosexual relationship has not yet been established and the thrust of adolescence is well past. Naturally, it will appear descriptively that the analysis has damaged the patient's potency, and only the patient will realise the contrary. The guilt about representing the analysis to the world, as it were, negatively, does form the core of a depressive attitude toward the impotence which helps greatly to power a thrust for further development toward genuine potency.

Discussion

It is impossible to separate the findings of psycho-analytical research into the individual mind from the cultural context in which the structure of personality arises. This is especially true when we are dealing with problems of high social anxiety, which often stand in a direct relation to the height of social visibility. The individual confronted with social values which run counter to his inclinations has only the recourse to secrecy or defiance. But secrecy, to be in tolerable relation to the values promulgated by beloved objects in the outside world, must be secret from the self as well. The device of splitting the ego, Freud finally decided (*S.E.*, 21, 1927) must be the chief device for remaining ostensibly healthy in the face of such conflict unresolved. This is undoubtedly true, but other forms of secrecy-from-the-self are possible without recourse to structural alteration. Of these, the creation-of-confusion-as-a-defence would appear to be the most common, or perhaps even be a general category under which the others, such as semantic confusion, con-fabulation, and retrospective falsification could be subsumed.

But the individual in defence of his inclinations may also be part of a movement of social change, whether he is conscious of the fact or not. Not that we are prepared to assume that every movement toward social change is on the side of the angels. It is even too early in the history of the two sciences, psychology and sociology, to know whether they study phenomena related to the same level of mental functioning. But it cannot be denied that the culture, in the form by which it is represented to the child in the person of the parents, makes a lasting impingement. It is quite impossible to say, on casual observation, whether an individual in rebellion is in fact activated by an awareness of injustice in the world or by *inter*systemic conflict in his own personality, made respectable, as it were, in social garb.

In view of the relative infancy of our science, it is merely a matter of individual intuition to adopt one or the other attitude toward the problem of "nature *vs.* nurture", which is really the problem of the extent of individual responsibility. If I adopt an attitude which is uncompromisingly on the side of such responsibility, its apparent harshness can only be seen to be mitigated by the suspension of moral judgement. It seems to me more useful to assume that decision operates increasingly from birth onward, as Ego emerges with its pleasure-pain-reality principle to dominate the repetition compulsion of the Id. Such an attitude places us in a position of very heavy dependence upon the conception of psychic reality, and of course the validity of this conception is in turn dependent upon the validity of our findings, that is, the degree to which the "facts" of "psychic reality" are truly "discovered" and not "cursorily improvised", in the words of Senätspräsident Schreber.

Argument

We appear to have followed a peculiar and basically unsatisfactory method of exposition for a work which claims to be scientific. This Chapter seems eminently open to the charge of tautology, starting as it does with definitions, which are then exemplified and further claimed as universally valid on the basis of admittedly limited experience and an imponderable attitude toward the individual in his culture. To make matters worse, we propose now to enter upon a logical argument. It will run something like this: since the adult personality is founded on processes of introjective identification with internal objects which are given their freedom, within the depressive position, both to combine and to retain their individuality, with special respect to their sexual functions and the meaning of these in regard to their parental relationships, the logic of introjective identification dictates that the adult part of the self will similarly strive both to combine with the sexual partner and to grant the beloved one autonomy.

What, then, are the implications of this logical argument regarding the thesis of this chapter: namely that ambisexual activities after puberty are always of psychopathological significance? The first implication is clear. We assume that the force of introjective identification with a combined object will create a thrust toward the establishment of a similar, but not identical, relationship toward a beloved partner, and that these partners will necessarily possess different genital organs and sexual qualities of mind. In keeping with the requirement of the infantile structures for integration of their objects, introjective identification will also manifest itself as a preference for monogamy and faithfulness. The third implication grows out of this second; namely that the bisexual disposition of the partners shall tend toward finding expression through mutual projective identification, employed as a means of mutual understanding and communication, in a non-omnipotent manner.

The third implication is of particular interest in regard to the differentiation of individual value systems from social ones. It is often observed that the creative person is the one with the "thorn in the flesh" and that conversely creative activity tends to fall off with the arrival of contentment in sexual union. But there are also notable exceptions to this dictum. I would tend to cite Herman Melville as an example of its validity, but J. S. Bach as an exception to it. How are we to explain the exception while still retaining our conviction that anguish, born of intrapsychic conflict, is the motive force which drives bisexual integration to express itself in creative activity?

I have suggested elsewhere that the depressive position tends toward the externalisation of the combined internal object on to wider and wider representation in the outside world, finally taking the form of equating the earth and sun with the parents, so that all the humans alive come to represent the mother's children, siblings, while the animal life and the dead represent her "internal babies" Depressive concern "for all the mother's babies" tends to express itself in acts which not only have the meaning of reparation, in the sense of Melanie Klein, but also of an activity which I have called "sermonising" and recognised as the motive force behind the "publication" (in Bion's sense) of works of art and science. This act of making public tends to have the meaning of giving birth and to be attended with all the anxieties and psychopathological potentialities of that situation. But I do not feel that it can be subsumed under the wider category of sublimation, which I will shortly take some trouble to abandon as a concept. My reasons are very simple indeed. This view of creative activity, that it expresses struggle in anguish, and publication, that it expresses concern, runs absolutely counter to the central implication of the concept sublimation, inferring as it does a by-passing of conflict as a defence against anxiety.

CHAPTER 17

Work, Play and Sublimation

As it was Freud's method to advance and retreat in his special capacity for deductive and inductive operation and also to hold on to terms and give them new meanings, the teaching of psycho-analysis always poses a problem in semantics which only an historical approach can resolve. Surely much of the schismatic trend within psycho-analytic circles is based on poor scholarship, one might say, in regard to notation. Another aspect of the problem is that terms, hallowed by antiquity, in our restricted sense, take on a life of their own and refuse to lie down and be buried in history once their usefulness has passed.

This Chapter is largely elegiac in regard to the honoured term "sublimation". Although it was used poetically in Draft L (1897) ("phantasies serve the purpose of refining the memories, of sublimating them"), it takes place as a technical term beginning with "A Case of Hysteria" (1905). "The perversions are neither bestial nor degenerate in the emotional sense of the word. They are a development of germs all of which are contained in the undifferentiated sexual disposition of the child, and which, by being suppressed or by being diverted to higher, asexual aims—by being sublimated—are destined to provide the energy for a great number of our cultural achievements."

It is clear that Freud is here concerned with social value judgements ("bestial", "higher"), with energy concepts and the hydrostatic view of the mental apparatus ("energy", "diverted") and with a biological view of development ("germs", "undifferentiated") which had not as yet found a basis for distinguishing between body—neurophysiology —and mind—psychology—as the field of psycho-analytic study. In this cleft stick as both biologist and sociologist, Freud ends by begging the question, pleading that perversions are not "bestial in the emotional sense" since they have an honourable origin in infantile sexuality, while, thanks to the power of sublimation, they may be "diverted to higher, asexual aims" and "cultural achievements".

In a postscript to the same paper, in the momentous description of transference as a clinical phenomenon, Freud distinguishes the two types, the "new" and "reissued" editions of earlier object relations indicating that the second is brought about by "sublimation, as I call it". "Others" (*i.e.* transferences) "are more ingeniously constructed; their content has been subjected to a moderating influence—*sublimation*" (my italics) "as I call it—and they may even become conscious, by cleverly taking advantage of some real peculiarity in the physician's person or circumstances and attaching themselves to that." (p. 116). This astonishingly astute observation is, of course, the rationale for rigour in technique, which I have discussed elsewhere. We are surely not meant to take these transferences which "cleverly take advantage, etc." as "higher cultural achievements", and yet it may be that the idea of the corrective emotional experience has its origins in this error, whereby the analyst, idealising his own "peculiarities" in "person or circumstances", attempts to use his position to influence the behaviour of his patient.

This desire to bring about changes in the behaviour—or, really, in the character as expressed phenomenologically—may have played too great a part in Freud's own clinical work at times, for it will be recalled that the "Wolf Man", in his later treatment with Ruth Mack Brunswick, complained that Freud had opposed his wishes to follow in his father's footsteps by studying the law, pressing him toward the study of political economy as a means of sublimating his homosexuality. Clearly Freud considered the Wolf Man to be of abnormal constitution, and therefore particularly urgently requiring sublimation, as the alternative to perversion or repression, to manage his sexuality. He writes, "What we describe as a person's character is built up to a considerable extent from the material of bisexual excitations and is composed of instincts that have been fixed since childhood, of constructions achieved by means of sublimations, and of other constructions, employed for effectively holding in check perverse impulses which have been recognised as being unutilisable." (*S.E.* 7, p. 238). It will be recalled that Freud insists, over and over again in the paper on Leonardo, the "Five Lectures" and the Schreber case, that the homosexual tendency to inverted object choice lends itself particularly well to sublimation and is a prime source of high cultural achievement, especially in the arts.

It must have been because of the zeal of his followers in regard to the promotion of sublimation that Freud found it necessary to sound a note of caution in his "Recommendations" (1912) on technique. "Another temptation arises out of the educative activity which, in psycho-analytic treatment, devolves on the doctor without any deliberate intention on his part. When the developmental inhibitions are resolved, it happens of itself that the doctor finds himself in a position to indicate new aims for the trends that have been liberated. It is then no more than a natural ambition if he endeavours to make something specially excellent of a person whom he has been at such pains to free from his neurosis and if he prescribes high aims for his wishes. But here again the doctor should hold himself in check, and take the patient's capacities rather than his own desires as guide. Not every neurotic has a high talent for sublimation; one can assume of many of them that they would not have fallen ill at all if they had possessed the art of sublimating their instincts. If we press them unduly towards sublimation and cut them off from the most accessible and convenient instinctual satisfactions, we shall usually make life even harder for them than they feel it in any case. As doctor, one must above all be tolerant to the weakness of a patient, and must be content if one has won back some degree of capacity for work and enjoyment for a person even of only moderate worth. Educative ambition is of as little use as therapeutic ambition. It must further be borne in mind that many people fall ill precisely from an attempt to sublimate their instincts beyond the degree permitted by their organisation and that in those who have a capacity for sublimation the process usually takes place of itself as soon as their inhibitions have been overcome by analysis. In my opinion, therefore, efforts invariably to make use of the analytic treatment to bring about sublimation of instinct are, though no doubt always laudable, far from being in every case advisable." (*S.E.* XII, pp. 118–119).

This then, despite alterations in instinct theory, was the position prior to the sweeping changes brought about by the "Structural Theory", as it evolved in publication after publication from "On Narcissism" (1914) to "Inhibition, Symptom and Anxiety" (1926). "We are naturally led to examine the relation between this forming of an ideal and sublimation. Sublimation is a process that concerns object-libido and consists in the instincts directing themselves toward an aim other than, or remote from, that of sexual satisfaction; in this process the accent falls upon deflection from sexuality. Idealisation is a process that concerns the OBJECT; by it that object, without any alteration in its nature, is aggrandised and exalted in the subject's mind. Idealisation is possible in the sphere of ego-libido as well as in that of object-libido. For example, the sexual over-evaluation of an object is an idealisation of it. In so far as sublimation describes something that has to do with the instinct and idealisation something to do with the object, the two concepts are to be distinguished from each other.

"The formation of an ego ideal is often confused with the sublimation of instinct, to the detriment of an understanding of the facts. A man who has excluded his narcissism for homage to a high ego ideal has not necessarily on that account succeeded in sublimating his libidinal instincts. *It is true that the ego ideal demands such sublimation, but it cannot enforce it;*" (my italics), "sublimation remains a special process which may be prompted by the ideal but the execution of which is entirely independent of any such prompting". (*S.E.* 14, 1914, pp. 94–95).

The application of this new orientation toward sublimation in juxtaposition to the ego ideal, later the super-ego, was further complicated by the new duality of instinct proposed in "Beyond the Pleasure Principle" (1920). The sublimation of aggression had hardly been touched by Freud (see his letter to Marie Bonaparte, 27th May 1937, in Appendix A, Vol. III, Jones' "Biography of Freud"). Furthermore, the equivocation regarding the source of the impulse to sublimate necessitated the further delegation to the constitution of a factor of "inability" of the instincts or of their "capacity for sublimation" (see Introductory Lectures, *S.E.* 15, p. 376). For instance, we come across the confusion in the "Wolf Man" where Freud discusses the little boy's "sublimating his predominantly masochistic attitude towards his father. He became Christ which was made specially easy for him on account of his having the same birthday." (*S.E.* 17, p. 64). This equation of identification ("He became Christ") with sublimation posed a problem regarding the nature of masochism which Freud only began to solve five years later ("A Child is Being Beaten", *S.E.* 17, 1919). But it also raised a question regarding the viability of the concept of sublimation as a move towards desexualisation and utilisation of instincts. A Christ-identification as a basis for character seems neither very desexualised nor very useful, even though, "It put a restraint on his sexual impulsions by affording them a sublimation and a safe mooring; it lowered the importance of his family relationships and thus protected him from the threat of isolation by giving him access to the great community of mankind. The untamed and fear-ridden child became socially well-behaved, and amenable to education." (Vol. 17, pp. 114–115).

What Freud has described was the inception of an exceptionally rigid latency period in the boy, acknowledging that fixation, ambivalence and partial repression of his homosexuality made it very fragile. "The only result of his repudiation of these efforts" (of the repressed to forge its way through to the sublimated portion, or to drag down the latter to itself) "was the production of apparently blasphemous obsessive thoughts, . . ." (Vol. 17, p. 117).

In "The Ego and the Id" (1923), Freud made a further attempt to resolve this conflict between the emerging concept of identification and the older one of sublimation. "The transformation of object-libido into narcissistic libido" (2° narcissism) "which then takes place obviously implies an abandonment of sexual aims, a desexualisation—a kind of sublimation" (*S.E.* 19, p. 30), or, "The struggle" (of the oedipus complex) "which once raged in the deepest strata of the mind, and was not brought to an end by rapid *sublimation and identification*, is now contained in a higher region" (between ego and super-ego) (p. 39); or "The super-ego arises, as we know, from an identification with the father taken as a model. Every such identification is in the nature of a desexualisation or even of a sublimation." (p. 54). But Freud goes on to say, "It now seems as though when a transformation of this kind takes place, an instinctual defusion occurs at the same time. After sublimation the erotic component no longer has the power to bind the whole of the destructiveness that was combined with it, and this is released in the form of an inclination to aggression and destruction. This defusion would be the source of the general character of harshness and cruelty exhibited by the ideal—its dictatorial 'thou shalt' ".

Thus in attempting to hold on to the concept of sublimation Freud was now suggesting that the super-ego *could* force identification upon the ego. But he suspected that this was a pathological organisation and could not serve as the basis of healthy character. The most advanced position of this thought on sublimation makes it indistinguishable from introjective identification and serves as a useful bridge to the views expressed and implied in this volume. In "Civilisation and its Discontents" (Vol. 21, p. 80, footnote) he writes, "It is not possible, within the limits of a short survey, to discuss adequately the significance of work for the economics of the libido. No other technique for the conduct of life attaches the individual so firmly to reality as laying emphasis on work; for his work at last gains him a secure place in a portion of reality, in the human community. The possibility it offers of displacing a large amount of libidinal components, whether narcissistic, aggressive or even erotic, on to professional work and on to the human relations connected with it, lends it a value by no means second to what it enjoys as something indispensable to the preservation and justification of existence in society. Professional activity is a source of special satisfaction if it is a freely chosen one—if, that is to say, by means of sublimation, it makes possible the use of existing inclinations, of persisting or constitutionally reinforced instinctual impulses. And yet, as a path to happiness, work is not highly prized by men. They do not strive after it as they do after other possibilities of satisfaction. The great majority of people only work under the stress of necessity, and this natural human aversion to work raises most difficult social problems."

The phrase I wish to emphasise is: "if it is a freely chosen one" (activity)—"if, that is to say, by means of sublimation, it makes possible the use of existing inclinations or constitutionally reinforced instinctual impulses".

It is relevant here to refer back to the clinical material in Chapter 10 which was used to exemplify the movement from dependence upon the super-ego-ideal at infantile levels to an introjective identification with their principles, "under their aegis" at the adult level of organisation. The two dreams of "the man in the sou'wester" and "Dr Ball's visit" demonstrated the distinction between *goals*, as an infantile motivational principle, and *aims*, as an adult one. The distinction carries also a fundamental juxtaposition, placing obedience to objects as an infantile mode, with its implied goal of reward by love and protection (including the infantile expectation of elevation-to-adult-status) in opposition to adult *faithfulness* to methods and principles—"under their aegis". This latter is the basis of adult work.

Since adult sexuality is guided by introjective identification, as explained in Chapter 9 on "The Introjective Basis of Polymorphism in Adult Sexuality", it now seems paradoxical, chicken-and-egg style, to relate the terms "work" and "sexuality" to one another in adult life. To take work as the wider term and subsume sexuality as a particular area of work would seem common sense, from a descriptive point of view. Nonetheless, in the realm of the meaning of behaviour as investigated by the psycho-analytical method, the term "sexual" appears to be the wider of the two, especially when its "parental" quality is recognised. Adult play would then have as its very essence the temporary relief from responsibility and work, in the sense that only one who works can have a holiday. It would imply something very different from the play of children which we understand to be turned inward, as are dreams, for the working over of internal conflicts.

The distinction between co-operation in analysis and self-analytic work helps us to answer the question of when the individual's work-life begins. Its coincidence with the onset of latency will be discussed further in Chapter 22 on "The Pedagogic Implications of Sexual Theory". In agreement with Freud, my conception of the beginning of the adult part of the personality would coincide with the movement toward the resolutions of the oedipus complex in favour of introjective identification. While it is true that the resolution at latency is both incomplete in mechanism—hedged by repression and obsessional control—as well as in scope—largely pre-genital in content—nonetheless the structuralisation of the super-ego-ideal from the multiplicity of part- and whole-objects in psychic reality is considerably forwarded at this time.

This massive movement toward introjective identification at latency utilises, of course, a mechanism that has been employed from the earliest times, for every movement from paranoid-schizoid to depressive position (Ps←→D) involves a movement toward introjective as against projective modes of identification.

I hope I may be forgiven quoting again the stirring passage from "The Economic Problem of Masochism"; "The course of childhood development leads to an ever-increasing detachment from parents, and their personal significance for the super-ego recedes into the background. To the imagos they leave behind there are then linked the influences of teachers and authorities, self-chosen models and publicly recognised heroes, whose figures need no longer be introjected by an ego which has become more resistant. The last figure in the series that began with the parents is the dark power of Destiny which only the fewest of us are able to look upon as impersonal." (*i.e.*, death).

This point, that new qualities become linked to the images of the parents but that the figures of the newer influences need not be introjected, was fully discussed in Chapter 11. In Chapter 10 the introjective basis of adult bisexuality was described for the purpose of distinguishing its polymorphism from that of infantile sexuality and of perversions respectively. In this present Chapter we have a different task in hand, namely to explain why adult work is so sexual, why the infantile organisation has an aversion to work and why the concept of sublimation has become redundant in the "structural" era of psycho-analytic history. It must be kept in mind always that we are speaking of adult organisation of the personality and not of "grown-up "individuals, in other words, that we are using the term meta-psychologically, not either descriptively or phenomenologically. We must relate play to work by relating each in turn to its relevant organisation. Later, the concept of perversion, in symptom and character, will be discussed in the Chapters on "Tyranny" and "Pornography" (Chapters 20 and 24). What we must demonstrate, or rather elucidate, is that the infantile organisation of the self places the ego in a primary relation to the Id, resulting in play, while the adult organisation of the self, through introjective identification, places the adult portion of the ego, in children and grown-ups alike, in a secondary relation to the Id via the super-ego-ideal, resulting behaviourally in work.

The first part of our task has been done by Freud implicitly in all his theoretical formulations, whether structural or pre-structural, and regardless of the theory of instincts or of anxiety, memory, thinking, or of economic principles, whether pleasure, reality or repetition compulsion. His picture of the plight of the ego in "The Ego and the Id" serving three masters, the Id, the super-ego and the outside world, is indeed an accurate picture of the infantile organisation. What it perhaps does not make sufficiently clear are the economic aspects, which could only be elucidated by the next step in the discovery of economic principles of the mind, Melanie Klein's description of the paranoid-schizoid and depressive position.

Her work demonstrated that the process of "idealisation" involved more than what Freud had described as an object being "aggrandized or exalted in the subject's mind". She showed that a process of splitting-and-idealisation is involved, whereby all aspects of the object connected with mental pain are split-off as "bad", leaving an "idealised" object. This is not the same as a "good" object, for its qualities so transcend the category of "human" as to imply a persecutory demand for perfection. In other words, idealised objects present very little that quality of forgiveness under which infantile thought-in-action, which we know as play, may proceed.

Where objects are still too idealised, confusion between good and bad may easily result, just as when conversely the splitting and idealisation is not adequate and fails to produce a clear distinction, in both self and objects. Under these circumstances play is not able to proceed because of excesses of persecutory anxiety and is either inhibited or replaced by concrete behaviour which is play-like in form but joyless and compulsive in quality. Delusions of identity due to narcissistic identifications, especially projective identifications, mar the childish spontaneity and inventiveness which the generosity and forgiving nature of good objects allow.

Under this hovering benevolence, the play of infantile structures enjoys an immunity from responsibility that enables the infantile ego to devote itself, in full egocentricity, to its developmental problems. The task of self-forgiveness, which is such a difficult one for the adult organisation when it does damage through mistakes of judgement, episodes of ill-will, negligence or ignorance in the outside world, is unknown to the infantile organisation, which finds total absolution in the tolerance of good objects and their reparative omnipotence in psychic reality. But just as psychic reality is primary and over-whelming in importance for the infantile structures, external reality and responsibility for the world becomes primary for the adult portion of the personality, in its introjective identification.*

Taken in this fuller sense Freud's description in "Civilisation and its Discontents" quoted above takes on a richer meaning in which the pleasure of work need no longer be viewed as desexualised in any sense. *Through the operation of admiration and introjection the "existing inclinations" and "constitutionally reinforced impulses" will*

* See my dialogue with Adrian Stokes in "Painting and the Inner World", Tavistock, 1963.

have found their rightful place in personality structure, as the qualities of the super-ego, unique to the individual, as described in Chapter 11.

Just as adult and infantile sexual bahaviour can often not be distinguished descriptively, but only through analysis of unconscious phantasy and motivation, so work can often not be distinguished from pseudo-work, compulsion, infantile omnipotent control and other forms of non-play emergent in behaviour when infantile, rather than adult, organisation has taken control of motility. No descriptive criteria will help the analyst to recognise these aspects of acting-out and acting-in of his patient, or of himself. Only the analytic method of investigating transference and counter-transference can help.

In the implication that all work is sexual in its meaning, we must acknowledge the affective aspect fully, namely passion. Its differentiation from the excitement of infantile sexuality is again too utterly subjective and solipsistic to allow descriptive distinction, but in our metapsychological language we may try to use these terms precisely, and further distinguish passion from fanaticism, rage, ecstasy, and other categories of mental pleasure, as has been done in the gradual elucidation of the many types of mental pain.

In the structural theory the affects may be given their proper place in the functioning of the ego and are no longer necessarily linked with the Id and mental energy. Their quantitative manipulation as an overriding principle ("Nirvana Principle") is replaced by their being subsumed under all three levels of economics (repetition compulsion, pleasure-pain-reality principle and paranoid-schizoid-depressive positions). The concept of sublimation, neither as a poetical image ("refinement of memory"), nor as a mechanism of defence (linked to reaction formation and desexualisation), nor as a consequence of super-ego harshness, is no longer needed as part of our meta-psychological system of notation. It may be retained descriptively, perhaps, to indicate those aspects of behaviour where sexual aim and object are obscure without the aid of psycho-analytical investigation of the unconscious motivation and phantasy upon which they are founded. Indeed, the term "sublimation" has long ago slipped through our scientific fingers and into general parlance, where its rather vague usage, sometimes implying a background of impotence or incapacity in sexual relations, does violence to Freud's original meaning as well as to later usage.

Just as Freud, in his later work, demonstrated the utility of the extension, in breadth and depth, of the term "sexual" which he had proposed in the "Three Essays", our psycho-analytic discoveries have now brought us to an even wider and most unexpected meaning of the word. As Freud's original neurophysiological frame of reference changed to a purely psychological one, the quasi-physiological idea of "psychic energy" has needed to be replaced by purely mental concepts of "meaning" and "vitality". While the vitality of infantile structures is derived from the Id and is manifest as a resultant of the play of conflict among the parts produced by primal splitting-and-idealisation and defensive splitting-and-projective-identification, the vitality of the adult part of the personality is dependent for its stability and availability upon the vitality of the internal objects. In its introjective identification with these internal parents, its bisexuality operates in the outside world at various levels of abstraction, but always with the same fundamental meaning—*parental*. This is reflected in our language usage of terms such as mother, father, child, motherhood, brainchild, seminal influence, creative, nurturing—and, above all, love.

What is true at the basic level of individual sexual behaviour is also true in the realm of character; narcissistic identifications which produce infantile imitation and perverse caricaturing, along with adult introjective identifications, shape the actual behaviour of individuals in the world. Small wonder that the individual person is so complex, so defiant of nosological pigeon-holing, so unpredictable.

CHAPTER 18

Structural Revision of the Theory of Perversions and Addictions

IT now remains to summarise and order the findings and theories related to perversions and addictions in the light of the structural revision of the general theory of adult, infantile and perverse sexuality. The chapter on "Terror" contains implicitly a theory of the metapsychology of addictions which must now be made explicit, while some of its social implications will be traced later in the chapter on "Tyranny". Equally, the chapter on the nature of the objects of perversion contains implicitly a theory, which needs relating to the theory of addictions, while some social implications will similarly be examined in the chapter on "Pornography".

Let us start by a brief definition:—Addiction: a type of narcissistic organisation of the infantile structures which weakens and may totally displace the adult part of the personality in control of behaviour. Its central structure consists of the "good" child parts having turned their dependence away from the parental figures toward the "bad" part of the self, initially as a retreat from depressive pain into the paranoid-schizoid position, but specifically as a defence against the experience of terror in relation to the mother's inside babies which have been killed due to possessive jealousy, oedipal rivalry and fear of weaning. The internal structure of the addiction consists of an enslavement to cynical modes of thought which desecrate the good objects and either expel them (manic) or bury them in the faeces (repression). Essentially *dependence* upon good objects is replaced by *passivity* toward bad parts of the self, in a mood of *despair*. In the process of this surrender, all mental pain related to the hope-hopelessness continuum is obviated. It is essential that the term passivity be reserved for this pathological mode of relation, and not be confused with the many variants of dependence, reliance, trust or helplessness which enter into good relationships, both adult and infantile.

This inner structure of the addiction can find expression in the perverting of any mode of relationship or activity whatsoever in the external world. It is suggested here that the general meaning of *perverse* be taken in this way as the basis of specific application. There is no human activity which cannot be perverted, for the essence of the perverse impulse is to alter good into bad while preserving the appearance of the good, in delinquent defiance of any judgement based only on descriptive criteria. In this way the impulse to pervert is related to the delinquent impulse through the wish to render the good objects helpless by virtue of their good qualities, such as slowness to judge without adequate evidence, generosity, forbearance, self-examination, readiness for sacrifice, etc. To the delinquent impulse the refusal of the good objects to judge in the absence of proof of evil intent is hailed as equivalent to a judgement of "innocent" ("They know not what they do!"), while the forbearance to punish is greeted as weakness, and the readiness to sacrifice as stupidity.

In other words, the bad, destructive, evil, satanic—whatever degree of malevolence may characterise this part of the infantile structure of the self in an individual—this part of the self is in eternal opposition to the good objects, in the first instance the combined object, breast-and-nipple, of the mother. It seeks to pervert the good relation of other parts of the self to the object and to bind them in addictive passivity to itself. To this end it utilises every means at its disposal: seduction, threat, coercion, confusion, intolerance of the good parts to depressive pain, to separation, to jealousy, etc. It seeks to pervert and to addict. And these are separate steps in a process extrapolating toward insanity and death.

The vulnerability of the good infantile structures to this influence depends on the adequacy of the primal splitting-and-idealisation of self and object. Where this splitting is inadequate, the destructive part has too easy access to the good parts to exert its influence the moment pain or strain arises. On the other hand, an excessive splitting-and-idealisation produces such a quietus of anxiety that growth is not promoted and the irresistible advance of biological development keeps imposing tasks upon a mental structure which is unprepared.

There is evidence in every analysis which penetrates into the depths and proceeds long enough, that the operations of the bad part of the self can be lessened in their effectiveness to pervert and addict by the establishment of a correct degree of primal splitting-and-idealisation. But further, Melanie Klein's thesis that the virulence of the destructiveness can be modified is repeatedly borne out. When integration of the good parts and good objects has been sufficiently strengthened for splitting-and-idealisation to be finally surrendered in favour of integration of bad parts of the self, a process is commenced, necessarily a very slow one, whereby split-off aspects of the object which cause mental pain to the good parts of the self (and had therefore been considered "bad") are brought into integration also. Thus step by step as the capacity to bear mental pain increases, the object can be allowed a greater integrity, which in turn increases its strength and its capacity to deal with the bad parts of the self. As those bad parts are allowed to move closer to the "family", their share of the good experience modifies their virulence and makes them available for integration to some degree in the constructive and creative activities. Nonetheless, it is inconceivable that the destructive part's basic opposition to the good objects, and its deep connection with the destructive instincts, should ever be totally overcome. Still, the power of the good objects should not be underestimated.

This brings us to the definition of perversion generally, and sexual perversion specifically. We are suggesting, as stated, that the adjectival form, "perverse", be taken as related to the impulse, as in perverse sexuality, while the noun "perversion" be taken as a nosological term for an organisation of behaviour whose metapsychology (not description, N.B.) is supposed to have the narcissistic structure described. We are then in a position to describe three *levels* of perversion, for which I am suggesting the terms *habitual*, *addicted* and *criminal*.

(1) The habitual perversion: this contains all the elements of the addiction's narcissistic organisation; the attack on the truth, the dismantling of the object to form the fetishistic plaything, the auto-erotic sensuality, the defence against depressive pain, the alteration of the relationship to pain into masochism by tricks of projective identification with the victim of sadistic phantasy. But it lacks the passivity that grows out of the defence against terror. It is therefore free to be attuned to the exigencies of external relationships and corresponds to the descriptive term "habituation" as distinct from "addiction".

(2) The addicted perversion has already become internal in its determination, and external factors have only a modifying influence. Thus stressful situations can aggravate, and contact with external objects which carry the infantile transference as "good" may temporarily relieve it. However, the mood of despair that it generates in the person's life is pervasive and a suicidal impulsivity is inevitable. The secret enslavement writes "insincere" to all other experiences and relationships except those of infantile transference and these are felt as too unstable or transient to fill a lifetime. Thus, while the adult part of the personality may continue to control behaviour in relatively non-stressful and non-emotional areas, these are experienced as empty of meaning except as a screen for the addictive perversion. Behind this screen the desperation, and its suicidal component, lead the person toward ever more dangerous forms and relationships in the expression of the perversion, aiming at being murdered by the destructive part of the self as an ultimate

mock-reparation, by law of talion. Particularly where the addictive perversion is socialised, its conversion to a criminal perversion is possible.

(3) Criminal perversions result from the splitting and projective identification of the good infantile part of the personality into a person in the outside world, most often, in childhood, a younger sibling. But it may occur at any time in the course of an addictive perversion when it has been socialised. If the typically oscillating enactment of the sado-masochistic game gives way to a consistent pattern of sadism and masochism, the active partner, in the descriptive sense, may find himself increasingly overwhelmed by the activity, metapsychologically. When this happens, the game begins to dissolve and violence is never far away. In lieu of violence against the old partner, the seduction and degradation into addictive perversion of younger "innocents" may be turned to as an overriding passion. This is in essence psychopathy, a category of psychosis in which intellectual judgement is unimpaired and moral judgement non-existent. However, it is always important to remember that a structure of the personality can be psychopathic or perverted, but a person cannot be a "psychopath" or "pervert" in any meaningful metapsychological sense. Therefore, there is nothing in theory to render these conditions untreatable. In practice, the problem of creating a setting that will enable a psycho-analytical process to take place seems almost impossible on an ambulatory basis.

This brings us to a special problem in the treatment of perversions and addictions, namely the perverse and addictive transference, which I will reserve for a separate Chapter.

CHAPTER 19

Perversion of the Transference

PRESENT investigations of this area are very incomplete indeed and in a sense we can hope to do little more here than to call the problem to the attention of other analysts. It is the problem that arises in all patients in whom perversion or addiction plays a significant role in their psycho-pathology. They will be seen to make a concerted effort at certain stages in the psycho-analytical process to dislodge the analyst from his accustomed role and to convert the entire procedure into one which has the structure of their perverse or addictive trend. As the subtlety with which this transformation is undertaken by the unconscious of the patient is of a very high order, its manifestations and resultant counter-transference are likely to escape the notice of the analyst until it is too late. That is, by the time he becomes aware that the government of the analysis has been subverted, this will already have become an accomplished and perhaps irretrievable, or rather irreversible, fact.

Since forewarned is forearmed, even the limited delineation of the problem that we can undertake at present may be clinically useful. In order to accomplish this I plan to discuss gambling, partly because it has not as yet in this work been given the attention it deserves in the field of perversion and addiction, but also because it affords a useful paradigm for investigation of the alterations in the transference relationship. Perhaps it would be permissible to use the outline of Dostoievsky's classic investigation of the problem, his own, described in "The Gambler", as a jumping-off place, since like so many of his works it lays out the anatomy and geography of personality with brilliant clarity. It was written, you may recall, in his later years, during the period when he had left his wife to run off with Paulina Suslova, was heavily in debt, subject to epileptic seizures and frantically repairing his fortunes by serially writing "The Idiot" for a newspaper, only to sink further into debt at every gambling table he encountered.

The story of the novelette is, in brief, as follows: Alexei, a penniless university graduate, has arrived in "Roulettenberg" as tutor to the two young children of the widowed "General", a retired colonel who, in the company of his courtesan fiancée Blanche, is awaiting the death of his wealthy grandmother to repair his fortunes, as he is hopelessly in debt to the "Marquis" des Grieux. With him is his step-daughter Paulina, who seems to have been handed over to des Grieux as a mistress in consideration of 50,000 francs, a fact she only discovered after yielding herself to his seduction. She plans to free herself from an addictive love, now turned to hate, by winning the necessary money at roulette, for which purpose she has her "slave" Alexei play for her. But he wins nothing until after the supposedly dying grandmother has arrived out of spite to provide a nightmare spectacle for the others by losing her fortune in a whirlwind of senile excitement. Upon her retreat to Moscow, Alexei promptly wins 100,000 francs, but when he gives 50,000 to Paulina to purchase her freedom she throws it in his face in a state of agitation and confusion, retiring to the paternal care of an Englishman, Mr Astley, who loves her, and of his sister. Alexei subsequently departs for Paris with Blanche to squander the fortune. The "General", now quite mad, is taken in marriage by Blanche for the sake of his status once she has cheated Alexei out of his money, about which he cares nothing. He is now a confirmed gambler eagerly anticipating poverty and the challenge of the roulette table, where, at one stroke, he might become "a man" again, as before.

It is of importance that the drama presented is potentially interminable. In regard to Alexei, for instance, a rise from poverty to "manhood" at the roulette table and subsequently to squander or be robbed of his winnings by a Blanche or des Grieux, this is his addiction, or addictive cycle. His winnings are to derive, by way of the roulette-wheel-breast, from the losses of a doting "grandmother"-mother whose trust and generosity toward Alexei in the story betrays her bemused love for her baby-boy. The maternal cycle is thus as follows: Paulina's mother, abandoned by her "General" husband who has been seduced and corrupted by the Blanche-Grieux couple, deteriorates (dies) and becomes the "grandmother"-mother whose sexuality and need for love is turned toward the little-boy Alexei, only to be drained by him until she "dies" in turn and must be restored by the good Astley-father so that, restored as his sister, she can once more nurture the little-girl Paulina.

Similarly the Colonel-"General"-Astley father has his cycle. Only the Blanche-des Grieux couple remains unchanged. Throughout, the two "children", the inside-babies, are in constant danger of being "ruined".

This panoramic view of the corruption of the oedipus complex, whether at genital or pregenital levels, whether part- or whole-object, is the view which gradually unfolds in the analysis of perversions and addictions. The combined object has been divided, desire has been replaced by excitement, the destructive part of the personality has seized control to create a narcissistic organisation. Unless such a personality organisation is continually restored by introjective relationships in the outside world—to parents, friends, a spouse, children, community agencies, religion, analysis—deterioration into psychosis is inevitable.

Freud noticed as early as 1914 that people whose sexual lives were deeply committed to perversions did not come to be cured. This is still true today and has been observed by many writers.* Rather, such patients find their perversion or addiction more real than their social relations and come to analysis with the intention of learning to modulate their total behaviour so as to be able to continue their habit or vice without danger of interference. Eventually, during an analysis, the despair behind this intention must be resolved and the struggle against the illness initiated.

But before this can take place an effort is almost always made by the patient to include the analyst and analysis within his way of life as the source of constant reparative introjection. The intention to create an interminable analysis is quite clear, not of a merely parasitic type but more perverse and more destructive. In both men and women, the analytic breast becomes an object of ruthless greed, whether the conscious motive is, like Paulina's, to free themselves from some indebtedness (depressive guilt) or to indulge themselves in perverse pleasure, like Alexei.

The analyst's susceptibility to this intention to pervert the transference, is of course, a counter-transference problem of infinite variety and complexity, but certain configurations can be recognised and are extraordinarily clearly indicated in Dostoievsky's story. The "General's" enslavement to Blanche represents the father's vulnerability to infantile sexual excitement, particularly of a masochistic nature, and seems to start the dissolution of the combined object. Male analysts are vulnerable in this respect somewhat more than women.

The dissolution of a combined-object attitude toward the patient favours vulnerability to the seduction for mutual idealisation in the maternal counter-transference. This leads to an optimism and generosity which sees in the most minute developments a hope that the analysis will soon "turn a corner". Women analysts are probably more vulnerable in this respect.

Added to these two counter-transference susceptibilities is a third, the danger of the analytic breast being perverted especially by the financial arrangements, into the roulette-wheel breast with its croupier-nipple—that is, mechanical and "scientific". The position tends to be sanctified by a very elaborate modification of the history

* See Gillespie, Khan, Balint.

of psycho-analysis. Justification is found for detaching it from medical science generally so as to deny that the analyst undertakes, first and foremost, to accomplish a therapy which will either relieve suffering, promote development, or, most happily, do both. The medical ethic of "nihil nocere" can then be replaced by the law of the market-place, "caveat emptor". This attitude of emotional sterility then alters the concept of counter-transference to imply that any emotional response in the analyst is pathological, neglecting to distinguish between healthy and pathological counter-transference on the one hand, and between conscious and unconscious counter-transference on the other. By this means the distinction between counter-transference phenomenon and counter-transference activity is blurred, so that the way is left open whereby counter-transference may be acted out freely so long as it is couched in the form of an interpretation, "I think you feel that you would like me to say . . .", with no evidence behind it but that of conscious counter-transference.

When this perversion of the analytical situation has been brought about, the total situation tends to become stabilised in the following way: the social form of the patient's life outside analysis is improved in "success" and "respectability" to a degree which would be described as a cure by the standard of social psychiatry. He is "well-adjusted", but his perversion is not yet "cured". In the analysis a certain current of cruelty to the analyst persists in demeanour, in missing sessions, coming late, grumbling about payment and mocking psycho-analysts generally, "present company excluded, of course". But the material is abundant, both as regards reports of perverse behaviour and dreams. Signs of collapse of hope in the analyst are greeted with triumph and accusation, while periodic optimism ushers in a perverse fiesta as negative therapeutic reaction. It becomes clear that the patient views the analyst-mother as being addicted to the practice of psycho-analysis, an analytical wet-nurse prostitute, either unable to get better patients or unable to acknowledge limitations. Only an exaggerated "detached" and "scientific" demeanour of pseudo-nipple-penis wins the patient's respect, even awe. He suspects then that he is in the presence of greatness, but is not quite certain whether the analyst is god-like or satanic. The analysis becomes a microcosm, replacing living in-the-world, in which the analyst is "fate", the inscrutable croupier-nipple!

This configuration, then, seems in my experience to be the hall-mark of the perverse transference: contempt for psycho-analysis (the breast) and awe of the analyst (nipple, penis or fæcal penis—confused). From it one can see arise the fetishistic playing with interpretations as whips in social perversions. Decadence of a psycho-analytical group would naturally follow this line.

Part III

APPLICATIONS OF THEORY

CHAPTER 20

Tyranny*

THIS paper has undergone three stages of metamorphosis beginning in 1962 when a conjunction of several experiences—some clinical material, a piece of sculpture, and a jurist's memoirs—galvanised a paper read to the Imago Group. The second stage was the working out of a concept of terror and dread, which I consider a supplement to Dr Bion's theory of "nameless dread". This paper was read at the 1967 Congress and appears above as Chapter 14. The present stage is an amalgam and development which both probes the social context of tyranny on the basis of psycho-analytical findings regarding internal tyranny in the perversion and addictions, but also aims to open the question of the social role of psycho-analysis, analysts and their societies in respect of these social phenomena.

Felix Frankfurter, the American jurist and Supreme Court justice, says in his talks with Harlen Phillips ("Felix Frankfurter Reminisces", 1960, Reynal), "I do take law very seriously, deeply seriously, because, fragile as reason is and limited as law is as the expression of the institutionalised medium of reason, that is all we have standing between us and the tyranny of mere will and the cruelty of unbridled undisciplined feeling".

This statement seems to me to epitomise the confusion between the law as explicit statement of the social contract and law as the rules for excluding and punishing the pariah. I have met this conflict in patients again and again at the threshold of the depressive position when the coming of trust and dependence on good primal objects is still so confluent with possessive jealousy in regard to them that punishment, even extermination, of the split-off bad parts of the self, in their projected representations in the outside world, is demanded as a right, a reward of fealty, a precondition of continued trust.

As penetration into the depressive position deepens, the function of sitting-in-judgement is surrendered to the internal objects at infantile levels and with it, by introjection, there results an ameliora-tion of the sanctimony. Who would not have been a Nazi in

* Read to the British Psycho-Analytical Society and published in the Scientific Bulletin, No. 24, 1968. Also as "Tirania" in the Rev. de Psicoanalisis 25, 817, 1968.

Hitler's Germany? Who can be sure, except the handful who stood the test?

Otto Fenichel ("Trophy and Triumph", 1939) refers to Engel's description of the Peasant War of 1525 and derives from it a far more ego-defensive implication than Frankfurter's idea of law. He writes: "In all wars, whether external or internal, there have been and are cruelities that are far in excess of tactical necessities and of the amounts of hatred actually mobilised in the single individual. Only psychology can explain these. Glover considers this to be a proof that deep-rooted instinctual motives are the true causes of wars, while what is ordinarily regarded as their causes were 'rationalisation' of these destructive drives. One can disagree with Glover's view without denying the existence of biologically founded pleasure in cruelty. One of the problems is that at most diverse periods the cruelties of war assume very similar and quite definite forms, in particular cruelties inflicted in order to dishonour the adversary. These involve either a chopping off of limbs or cannibalistic acts, or symbolic allusions to them. For instance, to quote Engels ("The Peasant War in Germany", N.Y. 1926), 'Many prisoners were executed in the cruellest manner, the rest were sent home with nose and ears cut off ... the peasants were attacked and dispersed by Zapolya; Dosa himself was taken prisoner, roasted on a red-hot throne and eaten alive by his own men, whose lives were spared solely on this condition ...' Now, these atrocities were committed not by the rebels but by the representatives of law and order; and one often has the impression that in the history of the world such things have been done more often and more extensively by the defenders of the loyal state than by the insurgents. It can be established that roasting alive and eating a human being is not prescribed punishment in any judiciary system. What was the purpose of this cruel command? To scorn and humiliate a beaten foe. And what determines the form of this scorn and humiliation? What was once one's own longed-for instinctual aim, but later on succumbed to repression, is imposed on others in mockery and scorn."

However, it is very evident that this imposition of the commitment of an instinctual, or perhaps paranoidal, crime is a far easier task than its converse, the imposition of the relinquishment of such crimes, on the one hand, or giving up of instinctual libidinal gratifications on the other. Amusing examples of the difficulty of western man to impose such restrictions on the Marquesans and Tahitians respectively can be found in Herman Melville's lovely books "Typee" and "Omoo".

Tyranny is not an expression of "mere will and the cruelty of unbridled, undisciplined feeling" but is a social perversion in defence against depressive anxieties. Furthermore, it is a social process for commerce in seemingly hopelessly mutilated internal objects. It grows out of cowardice in the face of the pains of the depressive position. The committing of tyranny engenders smugness and the submission to it generates apathy.

Clinical Material

The first three years of analysis of a deeply schizoid young man had been occupied with the rehabilitation of the internal parents with whose severe mental and physical mutilations he had become intensely identified. Only a secret, bizarre manic omnipotence had saved him from total despair. From early childhood, his ego states had been of two kinds: those dominated by his feeling of being horribly disfigured and hopelessly mentally deficient, and those private withdrawn states in which he felt himself a unique genius or saint, a figure of overpowering beauty and endless creative potency. The first state rendered him incapable of socialisation, partially ineducable, exquisitely sensitive to ridicule and helpless in the face of aggression. The latter state, in the sequestration of the family, brought forth a parade of delusional identities even as a small child: composer-pianist, commanding officer, news commentator, engine driver, and editor-in-chief. These, carried out with a brilliance of detailed observation and talent for mime, were hilarious enough to cause the family to overlook the delusional intensity with which they were being dramatised and the secret contempt in which the laughing adults were being held. In the complete isolation of his bed, a proliferation of masturbation into sado-masochistic perversions took place involving painful penetration of his various orifices.

The very uphill work of the first three years succeeded in sufficiently restoring the goodness and beauty of his internal mother and her breasts and the devotion and potency of the internal father and his genitals so that something resembling the analytic process began to take shape, with periods of co-operation, shattered by impending separations, and by negative therapeutic reactions following emergence of positive feelings whenever distant rumblings of depressive anxieties were followed by panicky retreats into omnipotence and schizoid indifference.

In this context, a monumental jealousy of the next baby, linked to his two-year-younger brother in the past and to the prospect of the analyst undertaking new analytic cases, began to dominate the separation situations. During the fourth and fifth years of analytic work, mutilating attacks on the genitalia of the internal parents, and on the babies inside the internal mother, occurred regularly in connection with holidays.

The autumn of the fifth year was occupied with two related types of behaviour about which he was very secretive. One was the drawing of pornographic pictures in connection with his masturbatory activities. The other was the evasion of physical proximity due to a delusion of smelling bad. This, he felt, was caused by a continual silent passage of flatus from an incontinent anus which he imagined he had damaged by his perversions. In the course of analysis, this latter problem began to alternate with outbreaks of vivacity and "passing jokes" at work and in the consulting room.

By the following February he had burned his pornography and toward the end of the month he was able to reveal that the pictures he drew showed women's bodies in various degrees of mutilation.

That May he reported a dream in which *he was afraid of the incriminating evidence on a piece of paper and, with his penis, was pushing it into his sister's anus. He felt puzzled in this dream as to why she was submitting to it.*

This illustrates the patient's devices for ridding himself of the mutilated body, the *corpus delicti*, of his internal objects by expelling it into the split-off feminine part of himself, projected outside, as a defence against the pains of the depressive position. Since the mutilated objects were by various means projected into other persons in his unconscious phantasy, these persons were felt to be burdened by the feeings and responsibilities he evaded. Smugness resulted, for the damage was not visible to him within his own inner world. All feelings of guilt, grief, remorse, and longing, were obviated. A feeling of total helplessness about reparation pervaded all such depressive anxieties, and the victims of his projection of damaged objects were therefore felt to be burdened with this total life-sapping despair also. Every orifice of another person's body, including of course the eyes, could be utilised for this penetration. Any product of his own mind or body could become the carrier of the mutilated object.

During the analytic work of the second half of the sixth year, a process of integration began very slowly to take place as a result of the gradually increasing desire to protect and preserve the beautiful internal mother, the analyst, and his external mother. The analyst and his mother represented the two people in the outside world who were linked to his good internal object.

It was a split-off part of the patient's personality that had originally inflicted the mutilations on his internal world. This part, because of its grinding relentlessness of destructive activity, had at first been represented in dreams only as machines—tanks, battleships, etc. Through the fifth and sixth years it had been represented in dreams and extensive acting-out by a cat, "Tigger", and it came to be known to us as the "Tigger-part" of the patient. By the autumn of the sixth year, there was occasional representation of this part in human form in his dreams, and its activities slowly began to reach consciousness. Earlier, they had been bound in the delusion of continual passage of flatus. Now they became manifest as a continual whispering on the couch whenever the analyst was interpreting, a whispering of cynical, ridiculing and abusive refutation of the interpretation.

The approach to the Christmas break of the sixth year was unusually successful in preserving the good internal mother and thus good feelings and hope in the analysis. Extreme anxiety about the analyst's safety and a deep misery of loneliness began to emerge into consciousness. In the last session before the break, he presented a dream in which *he saw a disreputable-looking negro asleep in a ditch in the rain. He woke him up, and the fellow then followed him as he went downhill, all the while pressing his penis against the patient's buttocks.*

The dream shows clearly that the destructive and now hated part of himself had been temporarily put at rest until the patient awakened its cruelty. It reveals that he was going downhill of his own accord; no one was forcing him. He wished to regress, to escape the loneliness, the anxiety of any depressive pains. The dream links with the one of his sister.

In February of the sixth year, after a very difficult struggle to restore the ground lost in his collapse over Christmas, he dreamed, after an analytic hour preoccupied with Eichmann and the Nazi extermination camps, that *there was a group of people of three generations outside the analyst's consulting room. They were shabby and starved, but singing and dancing with mixed gaiety and sadness. A young woman tried to take his hand and draw him into the group, but he pulled away and walked downhill. Then he was in his room, looking at himself naked in the mirror. He could not see his penis, but as he lifted his leg he was horrified to see that there was a third leg behind it.*

I interpreted, and he agreed, that he was horrified to discover that he had walked downhill with Eichmann behind him, as in the "negro" dream, allowing him to make an extermination camp of his internal world.

He was confronted with the choice of joining the human family, "the three generations", where sadness and gaiety are mixed, or joining the Nazis who hate and intend to exterminate all loving bonds among people. He chose the latter, by allowing the Eichmann part of himself to exterminate his good internal objects, that is, to destroy the basis of his capacity to love objects in the outside world, to feel himself part of the human family, to be concerned with the welfare of others. It is vital to note, however, that when he pulled himself away from the young woman who was trying to catch his hand, he did so to avoid the pains represented by the shabby and starved appearance of the group and the pathos of their entertainment. When he realised that by doing so he had given Eichmann dominion over his inner world and thereby sacrificed his self-esteem, represented by his penis, he was horrified.

This material was very vivid in my mind when I saw Ralph Brown's "Two Figures with a Carcass" exhibited at Battersea. It powerfully integrates the formal and emotional aspects of this material.

My view at that time was expressed in the "Dialogue" with Adrian Stokes published in "Painting and the Inner World" and was, I now think, a pessimistic one as regards the social role of psycho-analysis and analysts. It tended to shift the entire burden on to artists, or rather the "art world", of carrying on the social equivalent of the psycho-analytical method of interpretation with a view to lessening of paranoid anxieties and strengthening the bonds of relationship to good objects by which greater capacities for depressive pain might develop. Its hope was that the findings of psycho-analysis might percolate through the "art world", especially through the analytic treatment of artists. It might be said to have left the field to humanism as the heir to the church.

The hopefulness about the particular patient referred to above and in my 1963 paper on "Somatic Delusions" did not find confirmation in subsequent years' work, for his progress ground to a halt and has not yet been re-established. However, the problem which I could not penetrate with him was revealed and worked through with other patients and was reported in my 1967 paper on "Terror, Persecution, Dread—a Dissection of Paranoid Anxieties" (Chapter 14). Its findings were summarised as follows:

"Terror is a paranoid anxiety whose essential quality, paralysis, leaves no avenue of action. The object of terror, being in unconscious phantasy *dead* objects, cannot even be fled from with success. But in psychic reality the vitality of an object, of which it may be robbed, can also be returned to it, as the soul to the body in theological terms This can only be accomplished by the reparative capacity of the internal parents and their creative coitus.

"When dependence on the reparative capacity of the internal objects is prevented by oedipal jealousy and/or destructive envy, this restoration cannot occur during the course of sleep and dreaming. Only an object in external reality, which bears the transference significance of the mother's breast at infantile levels, can accomplish the task. This may be undertaken innumerable times without being acknowledged, if the infantile dependence is blocked by the denigrating activity of envy or the obstinacy born of intolerance to separation.

"Where dependence on internal good objects is rendered infeasible by damaging masturbatory attacks and where dependence on a good external object is unavailable or not acknowledged, the *addictive* relationship to a bad part of the self, the *submission to tyranny*, takes place. An illusion of safety is promulgated by the omniscience of the destructive part and perpetuated by the sense of omnipotence generated by the perversion or addictive activity involved. The tyrannical, addictive, bad part is *dreaded*. It is important to note that, while the tyrant may behave in a way that has a resemblance to a persecutor, especially if any sign of rebellion is at hand, the essential hold over the submissive part of the self is by way of the *dread of loss of protection against the terror*. I have come to the conclusion that intolerance to depressive anxieties *alone* will not produce the addictive constellation of submission to the tyrant, nor in combination with persecution by the damaged object. Where a dread of loss of an addictive relation to a tyrant is found in psychic structure, the problem of terror will be found at its core, as the force behind the dread and the submission.

"Until such narcissistic organisation is dismantled and a rebellion against tyranny of the bad part is mounted, progress into the threshold of the depressive position is impossible. Furthermore, until this occurs, factors in psychopathology such as intolerance to separation, or to depressive pain, or cowardice in the face of persecution, cannot be accurately estimated. The dread felt in relation to the tyrant is fundamentally a dread of loss of the illusory protection against the terror and may be seen to appear especially at times when rebellion has been undertaken in alliance with good objects which are then felt to be inadequate or unavailable, as during analytic holiday breaks."

In this summary I had not stressed a point concerning which I have grown increasingly convinced in the two years since its writing, namely, that, in the final analysis, these "dead objects" are the internal mother's inside babies.

Summary and Discussion

I have now presented an account of the development of my views over the six years 1962–68 on the subject of tyranny as a social phenomenon and have chosen to do so here in this way, because I feel that the call to action is altered and that the capitulation to humanism with its common sense can be reversed. Psycho-analysis is, I am convinced, the antithesis of common sense just as cynicism is its perversion, since it considers the laws of psychic reality, not external reality, to be primary. While common sense may appeal against cynicism in respect of enlightened self-interest, it can never plead within the depressive position without appearing weak and sentimental. It is bound to egocentricity, when all is said and done. It cannot conceive a realm of mind that is beyond self, as Freud has taught us to do with his discovery of the concreteness of the super-ego.

Psycho-analysts are therefore equipped with a theory, and with a method for using it, which can see meaning in human actions in dimensions of time and depth not available to common sense, nor to introspection short of the prophetic.

The theory of tyranny engenders foresight, and foresight makes action possible. The essence of this foresight is to be able to recognise in the outside world actions which are bound to have the meaning in psychic reality of the murdering of the internal mother's inside babies, where the paradigm of war and the concentration camp fails us in their delineation, and common sense gives tacit approval. Shall I mention some areas of social debate where psycho-analytical thought is required? The fisheries, methods of contraception, organ transplant, wild life conservation, divorce, drug taking, factory farming, vivisection, afforestation, archaeology, criminal law and penology, mortuary practices, safeguarding of libraries and museums, zoos, marriage, abortion, pollution.

May it not be that the tyranny and the ultimate perversion, war, is forced upon us by accumulations of unconscious terror and depressive anxiety constantly generated by activities which appear innocent to common sense, where we "know not what we do"? Perhaps only psycho-analysts have the method and material to delineate these areas and expose these activities.

CHAPTER 21

"Permanent Revolution" of the Generations

THE restless mind of the young Trotsky* caught a glimpse of the future of the Russian revolution and its predicament, that unless the new system could include as an institution the permanent urge to revolution it would relentlessly metamorphose into the monolithic state and betray its premises. In this paper I wish to demonstrate the sources of this urge to permanent revolution, to distinguish it from the impulse to rebellion, and to show its relation, in psychic reality, to the fact of the discontinuity in the generations and link to the barrier against incest which is fundamental to the human mind.

The basis for this discussion has been laid in the Chapters on "The Emergence from Adolescence" and "The Genesis of the Super-ego-ideal". But let us start here with the concept, so important in the early days of psycho-analysis and so little mentioned now, the incest barrier or taboo. The latter term betrays the anthropological inspiration to Freud's thinking and the way in which it was linked in his mind to the evolution of religion on the one hand, and the fate of the oedipus complex on the other. A more intimate understanding of the nature of childhood would incline us now to eliminate sibling relations from the concept of incest and limit it to the prohibition, the internal prohibition, against coitus of parent and child. This forms the background of the oedipus complex, resting as it does on the parent's refusal of the child's desire and the actual impotence of the child—the boy's seminal sterility and the girl's reproductive incapacity. We recognise the aim of the true genital trends in infantile sexuality to be a reproductive one primarily—to give and receive babies—rather than one of erogenous zone pleasure, as Freud earlier thought. It is the pregenital trends which, thanks to zonal and geographic confusions and distortions of identity due to projective identification, masquerade as genitality and carry the sensuous greed.

This unconscious situation at the heart of the genital oedipus complex, that the children cannot make babies nor will the internal parent indulge them in the attempt—this is the fundamental aspect of psychic reality which marks the gulf between the generations. While

* See Isaac Deutscher's Biography, Vol. I (Oxford).

151

in the outside world, collectively, generations of course shade into one another, the psychic reality of the gap makes itself felt continually in our modes of thought and feeling toward other people as individuals and groups. In a spurious way this seems to be most apparent where it is in fact least true, namely at the barrier between the adolescent and the adult community. The gulf that exists between those young people still held by the adolescent process and those who have passed into adult responsibility is in reality a structural one within the same generation. But in the unstable period of early commitment to adult life, a defensive rigidity of identification with the older generation seems to open wide a gap which is often fraught with sanctimony, akin to that of the newly reformed criminal, gambler or smoker.

For this reason the young father is more rigidly defended against the sexual attractiveness of adolescent girls than he will be 15 or 20 years later when his own daughters are adolescent and are busy reworking their oedipal conflict at their father's expense. The marital debris of that later period of strain on the incest barrier is far more apparent today than in earlier periods of history when the widespread incapacity to bear the frustration was institutionalised in prostitution, the keeping of mistresses, the acceptance of lovers, polygamy, handmaidens, etc.

The existence of the manifestations of this problem as a social phenomenon are far more common to men than to women; this testifies to the superior strength of the incest barrier between mother and son as compared to father and daughter. Here again newer understanding of pregenital development holds part of the answer, for we can recognise that the weaning conflict of the little girl strengthens her incestuous impulse toward the father's penis by addition of an oral component which is the basis of nymphomania; the boy however is driven away from the mother toward homosexuality. In this way the oral component of pregenital conflict seems, but only seems, to strengthen the girl's femininity, while it more obviously weakens the boy's masculinity. In fact, the highly ambivalent and part-object oral desires for the penis also weakens the true genital development of the girl.

Now, my point is that the true gap between generations imposed by psychic reality manifests itself in sexual choice, and of course in sexual conflict. But where a relatively satisfactory differentiation of adult from infantile has been achieved by people, the awareness of the gap between the generations is very stark, replete with loneliness and nostalgia. Who has not revisited the scenes of happy childhood memory only to find them "spoiled", no matter how striking the real improvement of the environment may be? There is a powerful longing to recapture the early phantasy of a hero's return to claim the birthright—the mother—in absolute possession, or, conversely, of the little girl to be claimed or rescued.

The adult experience of acceptance of commitment to introjective identification with internal objects carries with it a strong sense of being different from the external parents as well as needing to follow an independent path from the internal ones, be it ever so faithfully "under their aegis". What was looked forward to in latency as the inheritance of the world now appears as the responsibility for it, and it is a world which demands to change, to evolve, to improve its orderliness and experiment with new forms in every area.

Again we tend to feel that this may not have been so in earlier epochs, before God died in the outside world. Every old God was an aristocrat socially and a bourgeois economically, until he was replaced by a new revolutionary God, who in turn grew old, etc. But the pace was slower, surely—or was it? Perhaps the flux was just as great but more political, more open to the whims of nature, less technological. Perhaps human restlessness merely paraded as external necessity.

At any rate we can see with some clarity that with the death of God and the passing of the myth of eternal order directed from above, the death likewise of hereditary privilege, status and—gradually—property has taken or is taking place. From idealisation of the eternal we have passed, by way of the forlorn hope of dynamic equilibrium which even affected Freud's thought, to the recognition that everything must either grow—in complexity, in order, in form—or waste away. We see that the gap opened between the generations by the force of the oedipus complex and the incest prohibition is a psychic reality so compelling that it demands representation in the outside world. Politics today are becoming ever more clearly dominated by the struggle between the generations, while factors of sex, geography, financial and social class, religion, education and other variables of population distribution lose their significance for political alignment by virtue of the great fluidity of our situation or through the socio-economic irrelevance of the factor.

But defining the forces which open the gap between the generations does not in itself reveal the content of the gap nor its significance for external relationships. What has in fact been cleft in psychic reality by parental prohibition and infantile incapacity manifests itself in external reality as a discontinuity of experience, and therefore of communication. The generations do not understand one another, for they speak a different language—say, for instance, pre-war and post-war English. Every substantive word of the language takes on with the passage of time an increment in meaning and suffers a parallel loss. For words always have a current meaning and merely an archaic reference. If this is not apparent to you, go to see your favourite film of the 1930's, say "The Thirty-Nine Steps", the next time it is on TV or playing locally. Watch the rapt but puzzled faces of your small children and the amusement of your adolescent ones. Close your eyes and listen a while. Remember, I am talking of the language, not merely the words—the rhythm, musical intonation, diction, speed, vocabulary, coloquialisms, social distance, the spoken and unspoken message. All is changed in its meaning to some degree, at least as much as the clothes. The human relationships, you will notice, appear as romantic as the Round Table to your young children and as quaint as Pickwick to the adolescents. A heavy blow indeed!

Are we now in a position, perhaps, to put forward and examine the central thesis of this paper? I will suggest that the *political* population can, from the point of view of psychic reality, be divided into two distinct generations and three groups within each generation. There is first a younger generation, roughly 18–50 years of age, and an older generation, say 50–80 years. Within each there are three different groups, the rebels, the conservatives and the revolutionaries. Mind you, I do not cherish the illusion that *any* one person is always one or the other, but that as a population at any one moment they may be so divided. What is the psychic reality of these groups or *states of mind?*

Rebelliousness embraces all those states related to the height of the oedipus complex in which the struggle against the incest barrier is still in the forefront. It is characterised by contempt for the past, greed for power, resentment of authority, idealisation of novelty and disbelief in the importance of experience to the development of wisdom. It is dominated by persecutory anxiety and prone to violent means and the expectation of violent retaliation. It is determined to believe that the good people are being corrupted by the bad ones and that simple solutions and "final solutions" require only "courage", meaning ruthless destruction of enemies. Its aims therefore are always negatively stated, fallaciously argued and festooned with undocumented generalisation. Vendetta is the ethos and talion its rationale. Vital at 15, it becomes dangerously anti-social by 25.

Conservatism is the state of mind resulting from regression to latency mechanisms in the face of adult responsibility and the depressive task of working through the oedipus complex and accepting commitment to introjective identification with a combined object. Its longing for stability at any price inclines it to sacrifice growth and development just as it sacrifices sexual passion to comfort.

Being the product of introjective and/or projective identification with separated and desexualised objects, it is envious of youth, prone to equate age automatically with experience and therefore with wisdom. The belief in omnipotent control and balancing techniques inclines it to bargaining and compromise, while impaired symbol formation and constricted imagination render it at once materialistic, acquisitive and prone to confuse social roles with whole people. Its respect for titles and offices is therefore automatic, subject only to "checks and balances". Being unable to distinguish novelty from originality, it leans heavily on tradition to save it from confusion of values. Its denial of psychic reality impels it to see all events as "cause and effect" while even simple cyclic problems such as "chicken and egg" are viewed as mischievous word-twisting. It disbelieves the history of its own rebelliousness, for it has disavowed that identity and its unique development.

The revolutionary spirit arises the moment that introjective identification with the combined object is accepted as imposing a life of separateness "under their aegis". Knowing well how different are its internal objects from its external ones, it is resigned to the lack of communication with the older generation and prepared to find its understanding of the younger equally limited. Being convinced of the primacy of psychic reality and of dependence of thought upon the wisdom of its internal objects, it knows that its internal harmony is more precious if not more dear than any external relationship. Accordingly its allegiance is given only internally. However, it respects external objects, whether peers for their opinions, elders for their experience or the younger generation for its potentialities. Nonetheless, it is impelled by the inner fire of its interests and talents to pursue its own line of investigation and activity, welcoming comrades but waiting upon no ally. Its aegis dictates that psychic reality, and therefore motives and their attendant methods, are of primary importance and that aims are predictive at best and goals merely visionary. In following its methodological and ethical nose it is prepared for the worst, whether of sacrifice or to find itself in error. To waste the time-of-life it holds as a gift is its greatest dread and it is sworn, therefore, never to make the same mistake twice. However, it is not given to trial and error but rather to await inspiration, coming from its internal objects, and opportunity arising outside. It need not rush its fences as there are always other things to be done during the waiting, and it need not hurry its tasks, for there is much too much to be done however fast it may go. It is prone to work as hard as it can for the same reason and to look forward with delight to the coming of the new generation to which it will be able to hand over responsibility for the world, while it retires to retrospection and the quest for wisdom. It knows that everything it accomplishes will be swept away into history and seem feeble in retrospect, that it will inevitably have uncovered more problems than it will ever have solved. It is resigned to permanent revolution, not only in July and October but every day.

CHAPTER 22

Pedagogic Implications of Structural Psychosexual Theory

INDIVIDUALS are bound to have opinions on all sorts of matters and it becomes a task of introspection and integrity to distinguish between rationalisation of one's intuitive preferences and derivation of implications from one's theoretical convictions. The psycho-analyst's area of expertise is a very narrow one, namely the conducting of psycho-analytical treatments. But the view of life it affords is such a unique one, and so breath-taking in its vista, so sharp in its detail, than the analyst can easily forget the narrowness of method by which the other qualities are purchased.

Therefore psycho-analysts, even more than other scientists—and perhaps in this way like philosophers—are easily drawn out of their laboratories to sermonise, blinking in the unaccustomed limelight. What they have to say must be taken as compounded of concern, deep wisdom and practical ignorance, even where accurate drawing of implications has not given way to partisan rationalisation of intuition.

What is to follow is the distillation from lectures and related seminars for experienced primary school teachers training for work with malajusted children, given at the invitation of the Institute of Education of London University. The emphasis is on the age groups corresponding to latency (6–10), puberty and early adolescence (11–17), and late adolescence (17–25). In discussing the relation of choice of pedagogic method to psychosexual development, I want to concentrate on several different areas of education:

(1) skills
(2) information
(3) social integration with peers
(4) relation to authority and teaching figures
(5) thirst for knowledge
(6) imagination
(7) creativity.

It will avoid endless confusion if we discuss first how these terms relate to psychosexual theory, as this will define the narrow, but specific, area of meaning in each of these broad categories for which our theories of sexuality seem to have some clear reference and implication. For the sake of counterpoint, I will discuss them in pairs:

(*a*) yearning for skills; hunger for information
(*b*) hunger for information; thirst for knowledge
(*c*) thirst for knowledge; creative impulse
(*d*) creative impulse; imaginative power
(*e*) imaginative power; social integration with peers
(*f*) social integration with peers; contact with superiors.

(a) *Yearning for skills; hunger for information*

A certain degree of contact with reality is required in order that a child realise that size alone does not distinguish it from the adult world. Of the differences most easily perceived, strength and skill are most clearly defined, as distinct from knowledge, wisdom, creativity, responsibility, integrity, etc. But even strength and skill lend themselves to falsification, often with the playful connivance of the grown-ups, as exemplified by little boys "wrestling" with their daddies, little girls "helping mummy" with the housework.

Nonetheless, these two aspects of the real difference between children and adults are less easily denied or omnipotently eradicated by projective identification, with the result that most children, having clashed painfully with these realities at the height of the oedipus conflict, enter latency, with its characteristic eye-to-the-future, with a great craving to develop in these two areas, which appear to them to be so closely bound together. Note that their meaning is closely associated with the genital aspect of the oedipus conflict, in all its complexity referable to the making and rearing of babies.

In contrast, the hunger for information has its roots in the pre-genital oedipal conflict, in which the "richness" of the objects, at part-object level in particular of breast, tummy and testicles, is the item of special admiration and envy. While admiration for the mother's tummy-riches forms itself in phantasy of money, jewels, food or furniture, and for the daddy's testicular-riches in terms of armies, weapons, tools and power, the admiration for the breast's riches is formulated in phantasy in terms of happiness and knowledge. The breast, or really the combined part-object of breast-and-nipple, is felt to "know" everything and it is closely linked to the infantile image of the parental heads and eyes.

But the concept of knowledge is still formulated concretely as facts amassed and not as links, insights, understandings, points-of-view, etc. It is at this level that a hunger for facts and information is seen to exist in the latency child, often to a degree not distinguishable from hoarding and miserliness in the more obsessional children, but even in the healthier children the collecting tendency is clear. One consequence, of course, is the proclivity of latency children to learn by rote, to be satisfied in their curiosity at a naming level. To learn what something is called seems to them to imply all necessary, or even all possible, knowledge of the object, act or event. As philosophers they are little Realists. As psychologists they are Behaviourists.

(b) *Hunger for information; thirst for knowledge*
This drive of the latency child to amass information is very social in its nature and lends itself to competition, display, secrecy, commerce. But also, of course, delinquent forms of acquisition arise: theft, scavenging, fraud. Discrimination as regards value tends to be poor, just as the insight is shallow. Thus a child may eagerly memorise the names of football players or flowers without concern to recognise the objects visually. He may memorise a poem without concern for its meaning; dates of battles without any idea of human slaughter; names of capitals without any certain realisation that it is cities and not the spelling in capital letters which is involved.

Since the latency child is class-minded—for him the world is divided into adult (aristocrat) and child (peasant)—the tokens of aristocracy in dress, demeanour, privilege and information rank high in his index of desirables. The inner and outer orientation to social groups divides in an analogous way, into those who are adult-like and those who are still child-like in any respect. Thus the pecking-order type of class structure and snobbery from form to form in schools rests heavily on the awe of information. The school books of the next higher class appear to be so many holy tablets mysteriously inscribed by the gods. "They do joined-up writing", she whispers tremulously to her friend. "Square root!"—heart thumping.

But whereas the latency hunger for information is status-seeking, the thirst for knowledge of the small child, revived in adolescence, is power-hungry. There are mysterious depths to be plumbed, heights of fame and power to be achieved, by words and gestures. The great difference is that while the small child thinks his godlike parents know secrets, the adolescent knows that his clay-footed parents have not found them. Mythological heroes are all adolescent boys whose feats translate into cultural advance. Hercules the sanitary engineer of the Augean Stables; Jason the inventor of tanning; Ulysses the lawyer, inventor of tax evasion, legal hair-splitting and the plea of innocence by reason of insanity.

These secrets of nature belong to the category, in unconscious phantasy, of the inside of the mother's body. Possession and control of her, and therefore of mortality, are the ultimate aim of knowledge for death is felt to involve a mandatory return into her bowels, as life was an exile therefrom.

(c) *Thirst for knowledge; creative impulse*

This thirst for knowledge, then, is of a penetrating sort, not content with "answers" to questions, but in search of the tools to possess and control nature. Things have to "work", and be "proven". Knowledge is a sword that slays the dragon falsehood, frees the beauty of truth from the sleep of latency, or, more often, from the thraldom of vice and the satanic fecal underworld. It is a fierce, demanding thirst which knows that the secrets are there, locked up in the libraries, the laboratories, the minds of professors. Genius is the key that will unlock it and every boy and girl must be a genius—and may be tomorrow despite all the evidence to the contrary of yesterday. Wasn't Churchill a dunce at school? Didn't the ugly duckling become a swan? For beauty is to be got by secret, strength by magic, courage by artifice, wealth by the aid of Rumplestillskin and love in connivance with Mephistopheles.

This fever of puberty and early adolescence, this second eruption of the infantile-oedipal volcano, subsides gradually and the urgent vitality of late adolescence takes its place. The wild thirst for knowledge, having drunk enought to have discovered its own false premise, decides that the hero and the genius are not the same. The imperious wish for control of the mother's body gives way to awe of her incredible order: the creative impulse arises. Where nothing was thought acceptable before but to rule even in hell, a wish to serve arises—she, to serve her child; he, to serve his child's mother. Brain-child, flesh-child, child of paint and canvas, print or stone or human organisation. Broodiness and nest-building replaces the drumming of the mating display. Importunate urging yields its place to quiet, long-range planning. All need for display is counter-balanced by the dread of interference. Privacy becomes precious. And adult life commences. The introjective identification with the internalised parents has been entered upon, with its super-ego standards and its ego-ideal aspiration.

(d) *Creative impulse; imaginative power*

Still, broodiness and nest-building are instinctual functions; and a brain-child is a different creature from one of flesh and blood. The metamorphosis of the intellect from hunger-for-information to thirst-for-knowledge to creative-impulse is largely a matter of structure—of the surrender of obsessional defences, acceptance of oedipal pain, yielding to introjective identification and the differentiation of adult from infantile. The qualitative aspects of mentality involved are those caught up in the struggle between good and evil in the mind. But what of the qualities other than strength, goodness, vitality and dependability, qualities more textural than architectonic. Leave aside, if we can, the quantitative aspects of mental function—speed and complexity of data operations, if you can bear to think of intelligence in this Stanford-Binet way. We are left to delve into the nebulous area of talents, interests, passions, by which imagination expresses itself. It seems very doubtful that such talents exist latent in the concatenation of preconceptions of the infantile id, awaiting only the realisations of experimental opportunity to spring to pounding life. More often in the history of patients we see evidence that the qualities of external objects immediate to their developmental milieu impressed themselves on the infantile capacity for admiration and facilitated an introjective contribution to the qualities of the internal objects. It is true that the heroes of the pubertal child give definitive social form to these aspects of the super-ego-ideal, but their "anlage" can often be traced into the infantile setting.

Yet such factors only give form to the function of imagination and say nothing of the determination of richness. More precisely, unknown id factors and knowable experiential factors clearly play a part in the determination of a selective preference for one or another of the symbolic forms of transformation by which unconscious phantasy is made "publishable"—*i.e.*, available to conscious observation and therefore to secondary transformation for the purpose of communication. But the msytery of the variable richness of imagination, what can we say of it?

(e) *Imaginative power; social integration with peers*

If we turn to the function of social leadership, we find that it rests very heavily on the function of imagination, but in different ways at different ages. Leadership in group formation is naturally of two basic types, constructive and destructive, as groups naturally reflect either the extension of the concept of family or the embodiment of rebellion against it. The "good" leader takes responsibility for giving form to the defences against excessive anxiety and against the regressions by which the family is threatened, while the "bad" leader gives form to the defences against anxiety by which regression and abandonment of the family are implemented. In both cases the richness of imagination and the capacity to "publish" the formal representation of its products are the prerequisite qualities.

Psycho-analytical study of leadership in the lives of patients strongly suggests that passion and fury are the clearest indicators that

the conflict between the good and evil parts of the infantile personality has been joined. Creative passion and destructive fury fuel
the imagination alike. It is at the knife-edge between passion and
fury that the creative act of the artist takes place. It is to the
dramatisation of these battles that political leaders give direction—a
lesser form of creativity surely. Similarly in the games and play of
children artistic leadership may arise, just as political leadership may
structure their groups, their snobbery, their conspiracies. But
whether it is creative leadership in which the conflict of good and
evil is contained by the imagination of a single child, or political
leadership in which the roles are divided by splitting-and-idealisation
between two children, the power of the imagination and the gift for
communication will distinguish the leader (of the moment) from his
followers (of the moment).

Psycho-analytical experience with children leaves me in little
doubt that creative leadership is lacking, except for the most rare
instance, among children of latency, while it fails in its social
application among younger children for lack of communication
skills. But in puberty it reappears with force, equipped with
language, gesture, song and dance, ready to organise tribal life.

Thus in the latency period, social leadership is lacking in creative
impulse and falls to the lower level of imaginative power in forming
the repetitive naughtiness of the "baddies" *or* the bourgeois order of
the "goodies". In puberty the creative impulse, in its primitive
form, throws up the heroic leadership of the raiding party, out to
rifle the storehouse of sexual pleasure, jealously guarded by the host
of ageing parents.

We must conclude that imaginative power is the product of
conflictual ferment, at its lowest ebb in the quietus of latency.

(f) *Integration with peers; contact with superiors*

It is therefore apparent that imaginative power which determines
the child's orientation as leader or follower in any momentary
grouping of peers places him in a very variable orientation to
superiors at different periods of his development. The small child
will naturally organise with peers, within his feeble capacities for
communication, dramas of projective identification with the parents
in their various adult roles, all of them meaning to the child the
different aspects of their sexuality. Very little impulse to secrecy
colours his play, as it is not in rebellion but in emulation of the adult
world. His powerful oedipal yearnings draw him immediately away
from peer activity the moment an attractive adult is available.

Not so with the latency child, whose delinquent groups are highly
secretive while his bourgeois goodness is meant for display—on

parade—to the grown-ups as evidence of readiness for elevation into adult life. His "goodness", therefore, is characterised by docility, readiness to be taught, marshalled, tested.

How different the pubertal excitement! The sexually attractive grown-ups must be seduced and subjugated. The old and impotent —and thereby envious—must be defied. Merlin must yield his secrets before being imprisoned in the tree.

Pedagogic Implications

I have been discussing seven areas of mental functioning that have a particular relevance for pedagogy. It remains to draw together the age-relevant implications, again in the light of our revised theory of psycho-sexual development.

Young Children (say 3 to 5)

Moving from pregenital preoccupation toward the genital oedipus complex, they are little interested in skills, but are drawn on by a great flux of imagination toward play and toward passionate oedipal transference to adult figures. They are easily hurt by refusal of their desires and are persecuted by authority. This emotionality and instability makes them intensely rivalrous with peers for adult attention and difficult to bring into any co-operative activity. But this rivalry, coupled with a strong creative impulse, enables them to relate, as spokes to the hub, to individual tasks in an adult-presided group. While curiosity is intense, the thirst for knowledge is so concrete in its sexual reference as to be relatively little adapted to the acquisition of general knowledge. In fact, information tends to be so sexualised in its significance as to result in anxiety, inhibition and specific learning disorders. However, driven by emotionality, the yearning for expression in language, music, dance and graphic arts provided a rich opportunity for instruction by example.

Latency Children (say 6 to 10)

The craving for order and discipline and the urge to collect and hoard information renders the children of this age group "ideal pupils" for classical methods of teaching. This pattern is further enhanced by separation of the sexes and by teachers of the same sex. But while the younger ones are in need of such support against the continued oedipal trends, those moving toward puberty may often achieve a rigidity which resists the pubertal metamorphosis. This implies that early formality of pedagogic method and caution against excessive intimacy should be relaxed as puberty is approached. At that time demands for more imagination, individuality and responsibility would seem to be in order, along with information more germane to human conflict.

Puberty (say 11 to 16)

Although not always manifest in unequivocal manner, this is in fact the age of maximum mental suffering, characterised by confusional states of every sort. It is therefore a period of great turmoil in which the relationships to a "gang" or group of intimates of the same sex is the only balm. These groups have a very strong delinquent significance and pedagogic method does well to rely heavily on the internal binding forces of such groups and their capacity to work with rebellious ardour. On the other hand attempts to cut across these groupings evoke either destructive activity or insurgent inertia, pseudo-stupidity. The competition between the sexes is intense and meaningful, so that segregation of the sexes into activities considered distinctly masculine or feminine is resented, openly by the girls and by a more covert intensification of sadism by the boys. Contempt for information, traditional skills and old-fashioned methods creates an atmosphere of inertia. The desire for display, the craving for power and the preoccupation with beauty provide the best pedagogic hand-holds,when coupled with freedom for grouping and availability of an ambience for competition. In general, pedagogic aims with this age-group should be limited academically in favour of social containment.

Adolescence (say 17 to 25)

When the pubertal groupings begin to peel off into adolescent coupling, ambition begins to replace rebelliousness and the creative urge to rise in place of the more anarchic drive. Methodological guidance is therefore more in order rather than formal teaching. The firing of imagination, the freedom to pursue interests to the limit, inspiration by contact with figures of outstanding accomplishment, all favour mobilisation of talents, while rigidity of syllabus, mechanisation of examination and promotion of rivalry conduce to continuation of the pubertal pattern or a relapse, in the early twenties into latency sterility and narrowness. Continued economic dependence has the same effect. Methods of pedagogy which encourage self-criticism by virtue of the reality of the task and the concreteness of the product create the possibility of self-selection which minimises confusion and discourages pubertal egalitarianism. This implies that alteration of life plans must be feasible without social humiliation, though not without personal sacrifice. All systems of public ranking create an atmosphere of unreality in which snobbery proliferates fiercely. A sinecure is a death-trap to vitality at this time.

In *summary*, I have traced here the implications of sexual theory for pedagogic practice in relation both to the school as a locus of human relationship and to the curriculum in its widest sense. I have shown how emphasis needs to be shifted as mental structure alters with growth. But it is a description of emphasis and not of absolutes. I take it to be in essential harmony with the views of Whitehead and his delineation of the "rhythm of education". His components of the educational cycle—romance, precision and generalisation—have a very intimate link to the nature of the oedipal conflict, latency structure and adolescent organisation.

CHAPTER 23

The Psychic Reality of Unborn Children

A YOUNG woman, eight years in mental hospital for manic-depression psychosis, brought two dreams to a session. In the first, *she had some difficulty walking because there was a little pocket on the sole of her right foot which contained little sticks.*

In the second dream, *she had her head thrown back* (she stood up to illustrate) *and "sick was gushing forth eternally"* (gesturing with both hands in a way that made it appear that the vomit gushed forth from her mouth and circled in the air to re-enter her body at her genital).

As she rambled on in further description and association to the dream, it became clear that the sticks in the pocket in her sole were arranged like the bones of a little foot, "like phalanges", "falangists" (laugh). They were like the almond sticks with which she aborted herself the first time (when she was living with a fellow student whom she later married)—"What a bloody mess!" (said with vulgarity and callousness). "Later I thought I could have named him Karl, for Karl Marx." (The six months fetus was male.) "I was weeping and weeping yesterday and kept saying to myself, 'Hail, Mary, full of grace, the Lord is with thee. Blessed art thou amongst women and blessed is the fruit of thy womb, Jesus'. He'd have been 16 now. It's no use! Next week is Rosh Hashonah and then Yom Kippur!"

The next week she dreamed that *she was taken from her room and ward to the ward for old women and later she was taken to a place where she had nowhere to go.*

Here then is a picture of the structure of this young woman's despair: by destroying her baby with the almond stick she had created a pocket of sickness in her soul in which every bone of the baby's body had turned into a persecutor (falangist) murdering her Jewish-Communist babies (her six subsequent miscarriages) and filling her mind with the sickness that poured forth from her mouth as vulgarity and obscenity. She was on trial and would be condemned to death, to be taken from the place of judgement (her present ward and the analysis) into old age and thence to the place of execution. (She did not in fact realise that the death sentence no longer existed in Emgland.)

Freud seems to have been deeply impressed by the unbridgeable

166

gap between common sense and psychic reality, as evidenced by those banal events in the history of patients which gave every evidence of having functioned as psychically traumatic. He writes in "A Case of Homosexuality in a Woman" (*S.E.*, XVIII, p. 167, 1920), "One is also amazed at the unexpected results that may follow an artificial abortion, the killing of an unborn child, which had been decided upon without remorse and without hesitation".

Fifty years later we are no longer "amazed" but, rather, appalled that the common sense attitude toward abortion has so completely won the field despite the evidence which floods every analytic practice—and every psychiatric one which is open to the evidence—of the tragic and often catastrophic consequences of such intervention. The aspects of psychic reality which underlie these consequences are now well-known and it should be possible to lay down criteria in keeping with them for the guidance of doctors, patients and parents upon whom such decisions devolve.

Let us assume at the outset that the task is to enable the people involved to act intelligently and thus to carry their responsibilities in a positive manner rather than *faute de mieux*. It is not only the mental health of the pregnant woman that is at stake but that of every actor in the drama. In such situations the inevitable "buck" is "passed" to the doctor. Between him and the pregnant woman the ultimate responsibility, and upon them the eventual consequence, will most heavily rest. Assuming that a doctor acknowledged the danger, what is to prevent him from opting out by a blanket refusal to recommend abortions or perform them? One can only answer that it is a cowardly shrinking from his duty as there is no evidence to suggest a universal damage to mental health by abortion, while, on the other hand, there are mountains of evidence that the burden of unwanted children, or of desired ones to women grossly ill-equipped for motherhood, can be injurious or even set in train catastrophic events.

Similarly, for the medical profession to wash its hands of the problem and resign itself to legislative direction would be at fundamental variance with the ethos and tradition under whose protection (and prestige) we all work. Clearly the legislature can bind or free but they may not coerce the physician.

Or, again, to resign himself to the demands of the patient or family under the cynical assumption that they will only obtain a dangerous criminal abortion elsewhere if a legal one is refused, side-steps responsibility.

Granted then that the problem of abortion must ultimately devolve upon the physician and his patient, can psycho-analysis provide them with some guide-line to support intuition, benevolence and courage? Let us review the relevant finding concerning psychic reality against which the common sense facts of the pregnant woman's life situation and history are to be balanced.

The facts of psychic reality are these:

(a) a baby is, in the sense of possession, only the mother's baby. The father may in phantasy support its existence and defend it from persecutors, but its existence is co-extensive with the mother's existence—it has "always" been inside her;

(b) from among her many internal babies a mother is phantasied to "select" the baby to be nurtured for birth. And inasmuch as this "gift of life" is from her, its confiscation or destruction involves her in a task of mourning whereby the child is received back inside and restored to its place among her internal babies;

(c) dead babies which are prevented from returning within the mother by being buried in the feces, become ghostly persecutors, the object of paralysing terror, while their bereft mothers become the object of "nameless dread" (Bion), the typical "blazing eyed" mother of nightmares.

These, then, appear to be the salient "facts" of psychic reality. In the instance of any particular pregnancy and its proposed termination, the problem could be stated, from the point of view of psychic reality, "Whose baby and whose judgement?". In metapsychological terms, the question resolves itself into the simple distinctions between projective and introjective identification as the dominant mode of experience of the pregnancy. In so far as a woman experiences her pregnancy as her own, she is free to rescind the "gift of life" and to mourn. But in so far as she is in a state of projective identification with the internal mother, her decision to abort is equivalent to the "cutting-in-half" of the Solomon fable. The consequences are adumbrated elsewhere in this book. The gateway to regressive illness is opened wide.

However, a third possibility must be considered, namely that no pregnancy will have as yet occurred in psychic reality, at a time when it can already be established as a clinical fact.

Here then are the three questions to which a psycho-analytical consultant would have to offer an opinion if asked if he thought a proposed abortion was a danger to the woman's future mental health:

(a) Has the pregnancy been apprehended in psychic reality?

(b) Has it been construed through introjective identification?

(c) Or has it been experienced as a delusion of pregnancy through projective identification?

We would then have to consider the sort of data from which an opinion could be derived in respect of these three questions. Clearly in the case of a patient in an ongoing analysis the data would be at hand. In other situations, one could only establish a psycho-analytical setting, collect psycho-analytical data for some weeks and await the growth of conviction. In the meanwhile the pregnant woman will have had the unique opportunity for exploring her own thoughts, feelings and phantasies in the psycho-analytical atmosphere of suspended moral judgement. We can only add that it seems most unlikely for psycho-analytical questions (*i.e.*, concerning psychic reality) to be answered by non-analytic techniques of interviewing or testing. The final task, however, of weighing the dangers in psychic reality against the common sense area of social hardships and physical health, must rest with the principals.

CHAPTER 24

The Architectonics of Pornography

WHILE it is always a danger that psycho-analytic definitions may be taken out of context and applied unintelligently for obsessional control in the social sphere, the hazard must be faced if a guide is to be afforded, in the realm of aesthetics, to the artist and the serious scholar and critic for drawing differentiations of a valid and useful sort between the representation of passion in art and literature and its misrepresentation in pornography. This brief paper, one trusts, will be of no use to courts of law, Lords Chamberlain or compilers of one index or another, but may help the artist and his patrons to traverse with lessened anxiety and guilt the scorching borderland.

In my dialogue with Adrian Stokes in "Painting and the Inner World" I have drawn upon discoveries related to psychic structure to emphasise the necessity of recognising the individual and social forces which invade the art world for destructive purposes. I have attempted to reinstate the term "evil" in its juxtaposition to "good" to differentiate this realm of value judgement in aesthetics from the more technical realm of "success" in representation (or "transformation" as Bion has more recently called it) and communication. Such a theoretical structure in aesthetics, based on psycho-analytical concepts of motivation and responsibility, lend themselves to application in the consulting room only, for they are bound up absolutely with the psycho-analytical method for investigation of the mind. But experience in the consulting room should enable us to derive indicators of a structural, rather than descriptive, sort, for our external judgement of works of art as objects—aesthetic objects. ·

This paper is intended as an initial intrusion into this area, attempting to transpose a definition of pornography as a *calculated attack on the internal situation and integration of the self in other people*, *i.e.*, a motivational definition, into an operational and structural one which can be applied with some confidence to the work of art rather than the unconscious of the artist. As I have said, it is intended for *use* in the modulation and "publication" (see Bion, "Learning from Experience") of creative works, not for the purpose of harassment or control from outside of the "art world" as an organisation within culture. It would be an acceptable premise derived from analytic experience that only a person intensely involved in artistic creativity

170

himself would be in a position to accomplish the degree of introjective and projective identification required for the use of the indicators set out in what is to follow.

I was interested recently while listening to Aaron Copland discuss the work of Paul Hindemith, to note that his language was largely drawn from the visual sphere. While it is true that he was addressing an audience which could not be presumed to have an extensive technical knowledge of music, his presentation was by no means analogical but in keeping with the general impression drawn from psycho-analytical work, and recently stressed by Bion ("Elements of Psycho-analysis") that the visual image is the core of unconscious phantasy. This finding is greatly reinforced by recent neurophysiological approaches to sleep and dreaming in which the "rapid eye movement" (REM) phenomenon appears to be absolutely correlated with the dream periods reflected both in EEG patterns and immediate recall when the subject is awakened (Fisher).

Therefore, without slighting the other modalities of experience which contribute to the flow of unconscious phantasy, it seems reasonable to adopt the term "point of view" as a central mode of reference in the ensuing (Bion's "Vertices").

The next step in our discussion must be one aimed at orienting the concept "point-of-view" to the distinction between narcissistic and object-related aims in unconscious phantasy. From the developmental angle, the progress from narcissism to object-relatedness corresponds to the series of phases described by Freud and elaborated by Karl Abraham. But the dynamics and economics of the process have been opened to detailed investigation through the formulation by Melanie Klein of the economic positions in psychic life, the "paranoid-schizoid" and "depressive". Bion's notation of Ps$\leftrightarrow$D is intended to give force to the discovery that this delicate balance between progression and regression exists at every step in the growth process. It forms, in the dimension of time, a spiral configuration of no great geometrical regularity. This oscillation is studied with compelling force in the four time units of psychoanalysis, the session, the week, the term and the year, punctuated by the separation units (night, week-end, holiday, summer break).* Regressive movement (Ps$\leftarrow$D) is driven (*a*) by destructive forces (especially envy and jealousy) encompassed by destructive parts of the self (at infantile levels), (*b*) by excesses of persecutory anxiety stirred by destroyed or bad objects (internal and externalised), and (*c*) by intolerance to psychic pain (the spectrum of depressive anxieties) in good parts of the self (infantile and adult). Progressive movement (Ps$\rightarrow$D) is led by the good parts of the self (adult and

* See the author's "Psychoanalytical Process".

infantile) utilising the capacity for love in the sphere of the good objects (external and internal, ultimately the breasts of the internalised mother).

Following the lead of Melanie Klein, recent researches have convincingly established that the object of the "point-of-view" in unconscious phantasy is always the same, namely the inside and outside of the body of the internal mother, with special reference, under the domination of the oedipus conflict at genital and pre-genital levels, to the primal scene of her reparative coital relationship in psychic reality to the internal father, especially his penis, testicles and semen.

We now come to the focus of our discussion and a complexity which cannot be circumvented. Again I must refer readers to Bion's difficult but rewarding works with special reference to his concept of "thought" as distinguished from the voyeuristic process. As my ideas are not at the same level of preoccupation with the "elements of psycho-analysis", I must elaborate them in my own terms which, I believe, rest on the foundations of Bion's considerations. The "point-of-view" of "thought" in unconscious phantasy is directed toward "absent objects", whose activities and relationships are elaborated in unconscious phantasy under the sway of the anxieties and impulses dominant at the moment. This process, filling the gap in time when an object disappears from its place (Bion's "point") in psychic reality, contains a prediction of the state of organisation it will embody when it reappears—again, in *psychic* reality. This prediction and its subsequent validation in the inner world, while absolutely correct in that locus, comes also to be applied to the experience of separation from objects in the outside world, but with, of course, a degree of unreality which must be modified during development by the differentiation between the attributes of psychic reality and those of the external world. Its relic, one might say, is the concept of causality—a philosophical problem which need not detain us here.

In opposition to these processes of unconscious phantasy (Bion's α–process and Row C. See "Transformations") which comprise the foundations of thought, we must recognise processes (Bion's β–elements and Column 2 (ψ) uses of them) which again have their core in the visual organisation of phantasy and can be linked to the term, derived from descriptive psycho-pathology, "voyeurism". The crux of these activities is, of course, the refusal to accept the "absence" of the "absent object", and rather to intrude on its privacy by every sensual mode. Again I will insist on the visual organisation of the voyeuristic phantasy, for clinical data demonstrates that even when the sensual intrusion is auditory, olfactory, etc., the phantasy of projective identification becomes operative and "transforms" (in Bion's sense) the internal or external experience into a visual expression. Hence my cleaving to the terms "voyeurism" and "point-of-view".

Our next task would be the practical delineation of the characteristics by which differentiation between the "thought-full" and "voyeuristic" origin of objects presented for aesthetic apprehension can be attempted. But first a look back to the gradient narcissism object relatedness (or Ps↔D) might be mentioned for clarity. It is becoming increasingly clear that the crisis of Ps↔D, or the Threshold of the Depressive Position, in its application to the commitment to concern for the welfare of objects as an overriding principle of psychic functioning, occurs around the attempt to establish the dependent relationship on the *feeding* breast, at first as an external object and subsequently in psychic reality, as the infantile foundation of psychic life. During this struggle, which brings the oedipus conflict to its crescendo, the destructive parts of the infantile structure play a game, combining the technique of geopolitics and guerilla warfare, aimed at undermining "trust" in the goodness of the parental figures, fundamentally the goodness of the breast.

It is here that the impingement of voyeurism can be most accurately studied in the analytic process, and we would be pressed to predict that the impingement on persons by forces in the outside world is most crucial at times when this balance, on the threshold, is most delicate. While we can really only describe it accurately in relation to the analytic process itself, our reconstruction of development, as "growth", distinct from aberrant lines of development, would indicate that every step in growth must ripen, as it were, to this perilous balance (Ps↔D). From the cultural point of view and the impingement of the art world on the individual, we might also suggest nodal points such as adolescence and the mid-life crisis.

Now we can go on to the details of the investigation—which we can now, in a manner, dub as: the search for indicators to distinguish communication from "propaganda-and-assault" in the realm of art as a social activity and aesthetic objects as a part of culture. Again I must stress that this is not meant to imply a new tool for the fruitless task of distinguishing the pornographer from the creative artist in the outside world. Rather I am concerned for the individual artist since, as I will show later, it is at the knife-edge boundary between the pornographic and creative points of view within himself that the creative artist produces his best work. I am suggesting that the "illusion" which the artist creates is essentially a *view of the object from vantage point otherwise unattainable to the viewer*.

A deeply schizoid patient in his fourth year of analysis had two dreams following a very fruitful session in which I had been able more convincingly than ever before to show him that his masturbation damaged his internal mother and that her lifeless state inside him was the cause of his complaint of inability to take an interest in anything. In the first dream, *a girl he had known at school was showing him a picture of a cottage. It was a very pretty cottage but what he admired most was that she had drawn it as if seen from about twenty feet off the ground.*

In the second dream, *the patient was flying through the air following an open car which his brother was driving. When he looked down he saw his mother lying across the back seat of the car looking very ill.*

In these two dreams, despite the denial (the girl shows him a lovely cottage) and envious reversal (but he can see that his brother carries an ill mother inside him), one can still see the nature of his admiration for the analytic process as a way of listening, thinking and talking which shows to the patient something about his internal situation which is not available to him purely by his own mental processes.

Conversely, the process of projective identification from the motive of envy in order to have the envied object's point-of-view (the patient flying) is a theme extremely common to the psycho-analytical situation and by implication to the infant's relation to the breast and mother. It is expressed in the second dream, but the mechanism of projective identification is not made apparent. In many other of the patient's dreams he was accustomed to enter and ascend tall buildings in order to see the view from the top windows, often of breathtaking beauty (*i.e.*, seeing mother's body through father's eyes). It is of interest that this was also expressed in dreams and in daily life by his way of using his camera as a stolen eye.

To turn now to the operation of a creative point-of-view, I will describe some dreams of an adult patient. At the time, the analysis was preoccupied with the problem of the unconscious split in his attitude toward the female genital. This lay at the root of certain limitations in sexual potency and social attitudes.

He dreamed that *he was standing with an unidentified man on a ridge overlooking a valley with an estuary at the head of which was a harbour, village and outlying factory. The harbour's water was clear, but below a weir the water was muddy. He was thinking how nice it was that the tin-mines were once again being worked and that employment was once more available at the factory for the villagers. The other man said, "What a shame that the supply of leather has run out and the factory must close down".* His association was that a friend had confided to my patient that he had a leathery place near his anus but was afraid to see a doctor, who would surely think it was vereneal and that he was homosexual.

Notice that the implication is that the two of them are talking of different "factories", he of the womb and the unidentified man of the rectum. Note also that the weir which separates the clear harbour from the muddy estuary quite clearly indicates a division which implies that the boats in the harbour cannot go out to sea—*i.e.*, that babies do not go in the toilet. But in telling the dream this had not occurred to the patient. It was only the interpretation, the analyst's point-of-view of the patient's internal world, which revealed this differentiation, between rectum and vagina, between feces and babies.

In a dream three weeks later, *the patient was showing his wife around the grounds of his university, pointing out to her the two lakes, one above the waterfall, weed-choked and used only for fishing, the larger one below clear and used for boating and bathing.*

A patient, an experienced artist, produced the following dream: *he was at home and had a sudden violent urge to defecate. As he rushed to the lavatory, he realised he could not get there in time and seized the ashtray in his studio to defecate into. But his fæces kept coming and coming, and as they achieved mountainous proportions in the room, they appeared to lose their fæcal attributes and assume an appearance of chocolate ice cream.*

He reported an association that, while only a moderate smoker, he chain-smokes while working and can work as long as his cigarette supply lasts. It seems very clear that in order to work he must simultaneously rid himself of infantile idealised fæces, lest his creative work be contaminated by infantile manic productivity. I cite this material to elaborate the term "knife-edge boundary" as the realm of creative aesthetic activity.

We must now return to the central problem, of differentiating between the creative and pornographic points-of-view. I have already described the creative point-of-view and need only stress its qualities: it is obtainable only by imagination; its objects are basically the body of the internal mother, inside and outside, and her reparative and creative coital relation to the internal father; its elaboration in "publishable" form is motivated by concern for siblings; it makes no claim to be true in the sense of factual.

In continuing now with the pornographic, I will build up the argument step by step, introducing each step by a bit of typical clinical material upon which my convictions, or better, at this point, opinions, are based.

A schizophrenic girl early on in analysis confided her delusional system which, pieced together from the next two years of work, was as follows. She had been sold by her parents to a wealthy man who was using her for a gigantic research project on the treatment of schizophrenia. For this purpose she was confined to a movie set in which nothing was real but entirely composed of photographs for the sets and contraptions—or perhaps actors—as the people. She could tell this because none of the colours were natural, the air smelled artificial and the figures were discernibly lifeless.

But it also became apparent that her own eyes could function as cameras, employing various forms of blinking, and she often appeared with a minute bit of toilet tissue stuck to her eye-lash, whereby, from the abundant material referable to her anal masturbation, one could deduce that rubbing her eyes and rubbing her anus were linked— *i.e.*, cleaning the lens of her anal camera. She insisted angrily, when taxed with her creation of an hallucinatory analyst outside the window with whom she carried on a silent—or rather inaudible— conversation in the analyst's presence, that "Pictures are as good as people!".

From material of this sort one may deduce that a delusional system is a world of unreal objects created by misuse of the perceptual apparatus, under the domination of envy, intending to prove that this unreal world is as good as the world of nature, of both external and psychic reality.

A patient who was tormented, in his relations with women, by a continual state of excitement, dreamed the following at a time when his analysis had come to a standstill. *An advertising man, wearing dark glasses, was driving a horse-cart in the back of which lounged a lightly clad model, while the patient was following behind on foot snapping her picture. He did not know where they were going.*

A woman who came for consultation about her autistic child reported that during the delivery, while under light anaesthesia, she had had a dream from which she had never fully recovered and which so preoccupied her in the first six months of the child's life that she hardly noticed his gradual drift out of touch with her. In the dream she was taken away by some creatures to a place where there was nothing to do, which perhaps meant she was dead. And yet there was a little knob she could turn and occasionally it made it possible to hear what some person she loved was saying somewhere— for a moment.*

I conclude that the destructive parts of the personality are constantly attempting to lure other parts away from the sphere of good objects, into schizophrenia, by catering to their voyeurist impulses during times of loneliness.

A middle-aged author was somewhat disappointed by the reviews of his last book, written during analysis and lacking the sexual themes of most of his earlier books. In a panic he decided that he must have five weeks off from analysis immediately to devote to

* See Harold Pinter's "The Birthday Party" (Methuen).

location-research for his current book. It was apparent that this was intended both as a revenge for the summer break, just past, and as a period for secretly writing a thoroughly pornographic section of his new book. The night after this session, he dreamed that *he was about to take a rocket into outer space. It did not seem much like a rocket, but was shaped more like a book or tombstone. He had to cling to the outside by digging his fingers in amongst the pages while the crew, consisting of members of the Goon Show, were inside. However, at the last moment, it was called off: the crew lost their nerve.*

Like the artist who dreamed of "defecating in the ashtray", the patient was tipped in his balance between a creative and porno-graphic view in his work, by the abdication to the "Goon Show" parts of himself under pressure of various anxieties at various levels, but primarily in the face of separation anxieties in the transference. The dream shows also, in a graphic manner, the structure of a typical "untenable position" which he was so able to maintain by cynical arguments.

A 15 year old girl, coming after many years of analysis into possession of her femininity, long split off into a younger sister, dreamed, during her menstrual period, that *she was in New York buying perfume from a stand on the pavement in front of a big store. It was unusual perfume, for one inhaled it through an atomiser and it then emerged from all the pores of the skin.*

Several months later, expecting her period and looking forward with anxiety to her first dance, she dreamed, after visiting an exhi-bition of Aubrey Beardsley's work, that *she was standing in front of a chemist's shop. In the window were various sizes of red bags covered in lace, perhaps for holding cosmetics. A woman came up behind her, middle-aged, bleached hair and heavily made-up, chattering rapidly in French. The woman explained that her name was Marcelle, that she was a French perfume manufacturer who was exporting to England a perfume under her own name. She wished the patient to enter the chemist shop to purchase a bottle for her so that she could see if it was genuine. The patient did so and only realised on emerging that she had purchased for the woman a bottle of Martell—cognac!*

Here one sees a young girl's response, as if to pornography, to an exhibition. The French words have had the effect upon her as of a seducer, teaching her to use alcohol (Martell) rather than insight (the New York perfume) to deal with her sexual anxieties (of smelling bad, *i.e.*, confusion between rectum and vagina). After interpretation she associated also to Colette and to the "Gigi" type of phantasy, of being groomed to be a courtesan.

How far have we come? We have described (*a*) the integrating function of the creative point-of-view (the tin factory and leather factory dream), (*b*) the disintegrating and schizophrenogenic aim of the pornographic point-of-view (the "movie-set delusion", the "model-in-the-cart" dream, the dream of the autistic child's mother), (*c*) the "knife-edge balance" of the two in creative effort (the "defecating in the ashtray" dream and the "Goon Show rocket" dream), and (*d*) the correspondingly delicate balance in the viewer of creative work (the 15 year old girl's "New York perfume" dream and "Marcelle" dream after the Beardsley exhibition).

Conclusion

(*a*) The creating and viewing of works of art are both, and perhaps equally, hazardous occupations, as a duel-of-angels tension between a creative and pornographic point-of-view, delicately balanced, envelopes the transaction.

(*b*) I conclude that it is not useful to speak of any particular work as "pornography" nor of a particular artist as a "pornographer", nor any form of viewing as a "perversion".

(*c*) Insofar as it is a greater danger to mental health to seduce than to be seduced, the rule in art must be "Let the seller beware" even more than "Caveat emptor".

(*d*) The operative factors are so latent and subtle in the differentiation of the effect upon a viewer and expression of the motives of an artist, that the manifest content, or iconography, cannot serve as a descriptive indicator.

(*e*) Commercial motivation and related anxieties have a corrupting effect upon artists as regards the "knife-edge" balance.

(*f*) Since the artist's function is above all to use his imagination to create a unique point-of-view, methods which employ a technique that precludes the expression of imagination cannot possibly produce works of art.

Appendix of Central Ideas

Having dutifully constructed the usual alphabetical index, several considerations have led me to discard it and offer in its place the following index of the central ideas of the book. The more frivolous reservations were that it resembled an auction catalogue, the scavenger's delight and the author's nightmare. Furthermore it seemed a meaningless ritual leavened only by comic items such as "Bottom: see Mummy's".

The more serious concern was derived from the nature of the book itself, which seems to me to be essentially a reworking of well-established concepts in psycho-analysis into a new organisation of thought and tracing its various implications for psycho-analytical practice and the application of its theories to other fields. But it is also a very personal statement of the way in which I see these well-established theories and use them in the consulting room. It would therefore seem misleading to use purely technical language, hiding the new-wine-in-old-bottles aspect. I have therefore in the text employed quite a lot of colloquial expressions to imply the personal flavour being introduced to the old concepts.

As the essential historical basis of the concepts in the work of Freud, Abraham and Melanie Klein has been summarised in the first section, and as the references to other workers' conceptions is included in the Authors Index, no indication of other people's ideas is included in the following index of central ideas. Consequently, I have not included, either, those ideas of my own which have been published previously.

METAPSYCHOLOGICAL IDEAS

Dynamic Operations

Bibliography

Abraham, K. (1924). A Short Study of the Development of the Libido. Selected Papers (Hogarth), 23, 27
Breuer, J. (1893). Studies in Hysteria (with Freud), *S.E.* II, 4
Bion, W. R. (1962). Learning from Experience (Heinemann), 6, 13, 63, 66, 77, 92, 97
— (1963). Elements of Psycho-analysis (Heinemann), 119, 170, 171
— (1965), Transformations (Heinemann), 109
Fenichel, O. (1939). Trophy and Triumph (Collected Papers, Norton), 142
Freud, A. (1946). The Ego and the Mechanisms of Defence (I.U.P.), 90
Freud, S. (1895). Studies in Hysteria. Standard Edition (Hogarth) II, 4
— (1895). Project for a Scientific Psychology (Origins of Psycho-analysis, Basic Books, 1954), 44, 120
— (1900). The Interpretation of Dreams, *S.E.* IV, 4, 13
— (1901). The Psychopathology of Everyday Life, *S.E.* VI, 4
— (1905). Fragment of the Analysis of a Case of Hysteria (Dora), *S.E.* VII, 38, 120
— (1905). Three Essays on the Theory of Sexuality. *S.E.* VII ix, 13-15, 21, 63, 64, 82, 105, 128
— (1905). Jokes and their Relation to the Unconscious. *S.E.* VII, 4
— (1908). Character and Anal Erotism. *S.E.* IX, 22
— (1909). Analysis of a Phobia in a Five-year-old Boy (Little Hans). *S.E.* X, 28
— (1909). Notes upon a Case of Obsessional Neurosis ("The Rat Man"). *S.E.* X
— (1910). Five Lectures on Psycho-analysis. *S.E.* XI, 121
— (1910). Future Prospects of Psycho-analytic Therapy. *S.E.* XI, 5
— (1911). Psycho-analytic Notes on an Autobiographical Account of a Case of Paranoia (Schreber Case), *S.E.* XII, 94, 118
— (1912). Recommendations to Physicians Practising Psycho-analysis. *S.E.* XII, 5, 121
— (1914). On the History of the Psycho-analytic Movement. *S.E.* XIV, 37

Freud, S. (1914). On Narcissism; an Introduction. *S.E.* XIV, 37, 39, 122

(1915). Mourning and Melancholia. *S.E.* XIV, 38

(1916). Some Character Types Met with in Psycho-analytic Work. *S.E.* XIV, 43

(1916). (1st) Introductory Lectures on Psycho-analysis. *S.E.* XV, 5, 37

(1918). From the History of an Infantile Neurosis (the "Wolf-man"), *S.E.* XVII, 37, 39, 121

(1919). "A Child is Being Beaten": A Contribution to the Study of the Origin of Sexual Perversion. *S.E.* XVII, 38, 105, 123

(1920). Beyond the Pleasure Principle. *S.E.* XVIII, 8, 9, 43, 123

(1920). The Psycho-genesis of a Case of Homosexuality in a Woman. *S.E.* XVIII, 38, 166

(1921). Group Psychology and the Analysis of the Ego. *S.E.* XVIII, 123

(1922). Some Neurotic Mechanisms in Jealousy, Paranoia and Homosexuality. *S.E.* XVIII, 38

(1923). The Ego and the Id. *S.E.* XIX, 18, 64, 123

(1924). Neurosis and Psychosis. *S.E.* XIX, 44

(1924). The Economic Problem of Masochism. *S.E.* XIX, 15, 75, 105

(1924). The Dissolution of the Oedipus Complex. *S.E.* XIX, 17

(1926). Inhibitions, Symptoms, and Anxiety. *S.E.* XX, 76

(1927). Fetishism. *S.E.* XXI, 91, 117

(1930). Civilization and its Discontents. *S.E.* XXI, 82, 124

(1931). Female Sexuality. *S.E.* XXI, 20

(1933). New Introductory Lectures on Psycho-analysis. *S.E.* XXII, 123

(1938). An Outline of Psycho-analysis. *S.E.* XXIII, 44

(1938). Splitting of the Ego in the Process of Defence. *S.E.* XXIII, 44

Gillespie, W. H. (1952). Notes on the Analysis of Sexual Perversions, Int. J. Psa. 33: 265: 106

Jones, E. (1956). Sigmund Freud: Life and Work (Hogarth), 4, 14, 37

Klein, Melanie (1932). The Psycho-analysis of Children (Hogarth)

(1937). Love, Guilt and Reparation (in "Love, Hate and Reparation" with Joan Riviere, Hogarth)

(1950). Contributions to Psycho-analysis, 1921-45 (Hogarth)

(1952). Developments in Psycho-analysis (with Paula Heimann, Susan Isaacs and Joan Riviere), Hogarth

(1957). Envy and Gratitude (Tavistock)

Meltzer, D. (1963). A Contribution to the Metapsychology of Cyclothmic States, Int. J. Psa., 44, 147

(1964). The Differentiation of Somatic Delusions from Hypochondria, Int. J. Psa., 45

(1966). The Relation of Anal Masturbation to Projective Identification, Int. J. Psa., 47, 56, 67

(1967). The Psycho-analytical Process (Heinemann), 56

Money-Kyrle, R. (1961). Man's Picture of His World (Duckworth), 96

Racker, H. (1970). Transference and Countertransference (Hogarth), 9, 69

Rosenfeld, H. (1971). Psychotic States (Hogarth), 9, 97

Segal, H. (1964). Introduction to the Work of Melanie Klein (Heinemann), 55, 97

Stokes, Adrian (1963). Painting and the Inner World (with D. Meltzer), (Tavistock), 119, 146, 169

Sullivan, H. S. (1940). Conceptions of Modern Psychiatry, Psychiatry: 3, 106

Whitehead, Alfred North (1933). Adventures of Ideas. 164

Winnicott, D. (1965). The Maturational Processes and the Facilitating Environment (Hogarth), 51, 92, 105